Praise for Bob Cancalosi

If you follow the advice in this book, you will instantly have the advantage of two very powerful sources of inspiration. The first, of course, is the author: Bob Cancalosi is a 31-year veteran of one of the most remarkable leadership academies in the world, and a trusted mentor to top global executives. The second source of inspiration, however, might come as a surprise: it's you – the vastly more insightful and influential version of the self you are about to discover.

JOHN WISDOM
Senior Leader, Communications and Brand, GE Crotonville

I've always believed it was important to have an "idea system." Bob's approach takes this to a powerful new level. I've seen Bob's journals – his concept of Four Loop Learning is an idea system on steroids.

DR. SCOTT ISAKSEN
CEO, CPSB

The author's lifelong personal leadership journey has been guided and informed by his practice of journaling. It did not start out fully formed, but rather evolved over the years as it became a more useful learning tool with each enhancement. Through this book, and the journal itself, Bob Cancalosi allows each of us to start where he leaves off. It is a gift of infinite value.

DR. WARREN WILHELM, DBA
CEO, Global Consulting Alliance

Bob's unique take on personal development and growth through his powerful Four Loop Learning model is inspired by his own incredible journey, which shines through on every page. Inspiring and humbling, insightful and practical, anyone who embraces the learning from Bob's extraordinary experiences will reap the benefits for many years to come.

What Patrick Lencioni does for teams and trust, Bob Cancalosi does for individual growth and performance. His unique lens on personal and professional development through his Four Loop Learning model is both inspirational and practical — and is a must read for anyone who is serious about moving upwards and onwards, in all senses of the words.

PAUL SAUNDERS
Managing Director of One Step Beyond

Bob gives us a simplistic model for recording and assessing our experiences in life with emphasis on detecting patterns and themes that help us mentor and lead others, and personally have a more fulfilling life. Bob clearly role models his journaling and his leadership lessons with all of us. He is indeed a reflective force of nature -- in his heart, his head, and his hands.

DR. MARTHA SOEHREN
Chief Talent Development Officer and SVP, Comcast

Bob's commonsense journals are a testament for a life's journey without borders in leadership and relationships. His ability to synthesize his learnings and share with other leaders is truly a growth mindset.

ERIC K. JORGENSEN
President and CEO, JX Enterprises, Inc

Bob is one of the most passionate and curious learners I know, and he journals daily to build and refine his knowledge with one very simple and unselfish goal - to share with others. He has a compelling and succinct message on leadership impact based upon the principles of Four Loop Learning and his 30 year collection of leadership expertise.

DR. RANJAY GULATI
Director of Harvard Advanced Management Program

A dozen years ago I sat down next to a seasoned executive who proceeded to write notes in the most organized way I'd ever seen. I couldn't help but be curious, and that's when I found out that Bob's Four Loop system went far beyond good note taking. In a world where it's almost impossible to take time to reflect and learn, Bob offers a pragmatic, insightful set of practices to help you succeed and thrive.

DR. KARIE WILLYERD
CLO, Visa Inc.

I have known Bob for over 30 years. He has always been unusually disciplined in structuring and organizing everything he learns and discovers. It is exciting to see how his own personal practices have become the thoughtful and empowering Four Loop Learning system. Use Four Loop every day to unlock new ideas and energize yourself and your team to achieve new levels of success!

DAVID HANDLER
Vice President and General Manager, CMO Phillips

Bob Cancalosi has truly mastered the art of leadership growth using the novel approach of journaling. His method of self-reflection and Four Loop Learning provides a valuable template to allow both mature leaders and those in development to follow in the footsteps of this remarkable man. If you ever get a chance to meet him one on one or hear one of his keynotes, don't pass up the opportunity!

DR. MARK VARVARES
Professor, Harvard Medical School

Bob Cancalosi in my view shares that rare space of one of the most outstanding leaders I have known. What makes him so unique is his life mission to empower others by sharing what he has learned over his incredible career as one of GE's best leaders. He embodies what it means to be a truly transformative leader – open, generous, passionate and deeply invested in the growth of others – and in doing so has helped so many people win and thrive in their careers. Sharing knowledge and experience is key to driving performance in a team by building capacity in others. Teaching others, sharing stories of your leadership journey and what you learned is also one of the most powerful tools a leader has to grow and develop personally, and Bob embodies those very qualities that we can all learn from.

DR. RICK LASH
Managing Director, Kornferry Hay Group

You can eat from Bob's 31 years of studying leadership for over 20 years with 68 journals of insights AND you're "taught how to fish" for yourself from Bob's practice of Four Loop journaling.

MARK VACHON
CEO BlueCow Foundation

Bob offers a refreshingly practical take on journaling, giving leaders an approach to transform daily experiences into nuggets of wisdom to be shared. If you aspire to be a better coach and leader, Four Loop Learning is not to be missed!

APRIL DUNN
Chief Marketing Officer, Manpower Group

It is a well-done, intriguing, comprehensive, and very effective method for gaining more insight and focus from the rich experiences that most often simply pass with little serious reflection. More than a management tool, Four Loop learning provides self-awareness, increased focus and effectiveness, and a greater appreciation for what makes life special.

GREG CARPENTER
Professor of Marketing, Kellogg School, Northwestern University

Story telling is a powerful way to share learning throughout your organization as the relevant points can really stick for a long time. Journaling provides you with a tool to record, reflect and refine the messages you want to share to generate the optimal story. The messages we share as leaders have to be almost impossible to misunderstand. The art of journaling can help create and connect the critical points to help keep your organization aligned on the most important things. The Four Loop Learning process is a proven tool to support the creating of compelling stories.

JOSEPH HOGAN
CEO, Align Technology, Inc.

Bob Cancalosi takes readers on an inspired journey into his vulnerable, unselfish, caring and authentic lived and leadership experience. This is not just a splendid book about "Deliberate Reflection", it is a spectacular one that inspires you not only to step back from and analyze your learning experience but to learn about yourself to lift your future performance as an incomparable leader.

DR. SYDNEY SAVION
CLO, New Zealand Airlines

I've kept a notebook (journal) with me since I joined Corporate America about 30 years ago. Initially, it was because I was right out of my graduate program, beginning my first professional job, and felt like I needed a way to keep track of all the data that was coming at me faster than I could process it. As my career progressed, I realized "journaling" had become a natural part of how

I captured, synthesized and learned how to keep learning. By occasionally reflecting on the notes I had written (new ideas, concepts, thoughts, etc.) it provided a mechanism to reconnect my head, heart and hand to what I had considered important at that moment in time. I also found it was a great way to re-energize. Whether consciously or subconsciously what I captured in my notes tended to be things that reconnected me back to my sense of purpose and passion in life. What I appreciate about Bob's approach, is that he's designed a methodology directly into the journal that elicits self-reflection in a focused and mindful way. You're encouraged to continually assess, edit and prioritize your thoughts, which provides greater clarity, deeper learning and commitment to action.

JOHN WADDELL
CLO, Zimmerbiomet

The years I have spent working with Bob on his health, he has spent teaching me how to be a better doctor, a more effective speaker, and a more aware learner of lessons from all of my patients. Like Bob, I deeply care about the people I work with, but his FOUR LOOP METHOD, particularly the fourth loop of sharing, helped me see that sharing is inherently reciprocal: when my patients feel that they can share their knowledge with me, the therapeutic relationship deepens, and my expertise expands exponentially.

CARRIE MURPHY, LAC
Doctor of Acupuncture and Chinese Medicine

Bob's journaling playbook is an incredible gift! I share it with all my placements. I wish I would have started years ago.

STEPHEN G. PATSCOT
Partner, Spencer Stuart

Through Bob's incredible art of journaling and extraordinary leadership models, I have learned the exhilarating power, impact, and fulfillment of reflection. As a curious learner with an interest in the continuous cultivation of my leadership skills, journaling has made me realize that every day starts and ends with me- my goals, my beliefs, my passions, my words, and my actions. I have learned that there is no better way to find these ambitions, thoughts, or words than through the act of journaling to refine my desires, my actions, and ultimately my impact on those around me. Bob Cancalosi's Leadership Reflections is the start to the journey of strengthening who you are, what's important to you, how you want to evolve, and what lessons you want to take away from your life experiences.

SAMANTHA ZARRINI
GE Corporate- Digital Programs Mentee

The Art of Journaling
FOUR LOOP LEARNING™
& Reflective Leadership

BOB CANCALOSI

Illustrations by Julianne Cancalosi

Copyright © 2019 First edition by Bob Cancalosi
All rights reserved.

TO: FOUR LOOP LEARNING- The Art of Journaling and Reflective Leadership
Author: Bob Cancalosi

www.fourlooplearning.com

Cover Design and Illustrations: Julianne Cancalosi
Back Cover Photo by Jeff Engel

No part of this publication may be reproduced, stored in a retrieval system, or transmitted in any form or by any means, electronic, mechanical, photocopying, recording, scanning, or otherwise, except as permitted under section 107 or 108 of the 1976 United States Copyright Act, without either the prior written permission of the author, Bob Cancalosi.

Limit of Liability/Disclaimer of Warranty: While the author has done his best efforts in preparing this book, he makes no representation of warranties with respect to the accuracy or completeness of the contents of this book and specifically disclaim any implied warranties of merchantability or fitness to a particular purpose.

ISBN: 978-1-61244-742-1
Library of Congress Control Number: 2019903595

Printed in the United States of America

Published by Halo Publishing International
1100 NW Loop 410
Suite 700 - 176
San Antonio, Texas 78213
www.halopublishing.com
contact@halopublishing.com

Dedication

This book is dedicated to my family:

To my wife Barbara for being by my side every day on every step of our unexpected medical journey, and for constantly encouraging me to share my gifts with others and pursue my ambition.

To my daughter Julianne who created all of the custom graphics in the book and the Leadership Reflections Journal. I learned from Julianne that any worthwhile pursuit in life should have a graphical representation.

To my son Jack who reminded me the importance of word choice and context in writing a compelling message. I learned from Jack to never forget that knowing my audience and what they care about is the most important context needed.

To my daughter Ali who inspired me to follow my dreams and spend the most amount of time doing what I love. I learned from Ali the healing power of optimistic thinking and to "Bee" Positive.

And finally, to my two standard poodles who constantly pawed me for attention while I wrote this book. I learned from them the value of companionship and the comfort of having them by my side throughout my journey.

CONTENTS

FOREWORD	14
MY JOURNEY INTO FOUR LOOP LEARNING	20
THE ACT OF SHARING	26
WHAT IS JOURNALING?	34
THE FOUR LOOPS OF LEARNING	50
LOOP 1: RECORD	56
LOOP 2: REFLECT	70
LOOP 3: ACT	92
LOOP 4: SHARE	104
SETTING UP YOUR JOURNAL	114
CONCLUSION	118

Foreword:

THE EVOLUTION OF AN IDEA AND A LEADER

By Joel Serra, J.D., Director of Safety Programs, Heli-Ski USA

When I first met Bob Cancalosi in the summer of 1980 he had hair long enough to have been comfortable at Woodstock and enough energy to power the lights on a Broadway marquee. The long hair disappeared many years ago and what's left doesn't cover all the available real estate, but the energy remains and that's what strikes home as you meet Bob. Pure and clean, undeniable and magnetic, energy that makes you want to stop and hear what he has to say.

We were both transfer students at St. Bonaventure University, majoring in Management Science, though some people thought that Bob was really majoring in soccer. The following season his teammates voted him captain – quite an achievement after only one year on the team. What quickly became apparent was that whether kicking a ball on a grassy field or brainstorming for better answers on group projects assigned as part of our management curriculum, you wanted Bob on your team. He had more creative ideas than a dorm full of marketing students. They weren't always good ideas, but the rest of us struggled to write them down before they were lost under the avalanche of ideas that followed. But how do you capture and direct all that energy?

> "THE REAL SECRET OF THE JOURNALING IS IN THE DISCIPLINE IT CREATES. INSTEAD OF REACTING TO PROBLEMS AND SEEMINGLY ENDLESS CRISES, JOURNALING CREATES THE SPACE TO LEARN FROM WHERE WE'VE BEEN AND THEN TO ANTICIPATE WHAT WILL LIKELY FOLLOW."
>
> — JOEL SERRA

Four Loop Learning: The Art of Journaling and Reflective Leadership

It was the spring of 1982 around 11:00 on a Friday night and we were standing against the wall in the campus pub, holding onto our beers and trying to have a conversation over the cacophony of loud music and four or five hundred students trying to do more or less the same thing. The details of the conversation are long forgotten, but I recall that we were trying to come up with a unique strategy for our final group project in a class that the School of Business referred to as the "Capstone" of our management curriculum. Graduation loomed large on the horizon. "Let's get out of here" Bob said, "I'm going deaf, my throat hurts from shouting and I need some air." We adjourned to some fresh air and an opportunity to think as we walked toward the off-campus trailer that I called home and a smaller party that was undoubtedly going on there. An easier place to talk, but still low on fresh air. "Let's take your canoe out for a float," Bob said. It was nearing midnight and the Allegany River was in flood, literally right in my backyard. Like I said, they weren't always good ideas.

You're probably thinking, "who brings a canoe to college?" Ok, I'm a bit of a geek, but also enough of a geek to insist that we wear life jackets. One good idea – perhaps this wasn't an entirely reckless endeavor. As we pushed off into a large back-eddy that existed only because of the flood, a fence of large trees stood between us and the main river channel and a full moon gave just enough light to see the hazards we needed to avoid. After some tense moments, we realized that we could paddle up the numerous back eddies, making upstream progress with little effort and resolving one problem – how do we get back where we started from? It wasn't that we hadn't thought about it, we just decided that the prospect of a long walk back wasn't reason enough to kill a promising adventure.

Paddling in the dark helps to focus one's thoughts. The rhythm of paddle strokes becomes unthinking, a metronome like cadence that quiets the mind. Darkness takes away the distractions that can derail a thought, a conversation or an inspired idea. And the inspired

Foreword

ideas began to flow. The first defined everything that came afterward: what we delivered in the classroom presentation had to be original – it couldn't look like anything another group might present. As Bob began to verbalize his vision for our project I was able to help to shape it with a few ideas of my own, but more often with questions that helped to put a structure around that vision.

After perhaps an hour of discussion and slow paddling, we ran out of eddies; we were up against the high bank that signaled we were behind the University's athletic fields. Decision time: cross the main channel of the river to find more eddies to climb further up-stream or call an end to this adventure? The obvious but nearly invisible hazard: floating trees and other debris loosened from the banks by the flood stage river. A moment's thought, a short conversation, a decision and we were ferrying across the current to the far bank and into the flooded farm fields beyond. More exploration and more discussion. Somewhere around 3 AM we paddled back into my yard with a solid idea about how to approach our project. It didn't take much selling – our fellow group members liked the idea and together we ran with it to the smiling approval of our classmates and professor.

We couldn't possibly have known at the time, but the work we were to undertake in the corporate world was always more complex, the personalities, talents and predilections of coworkers much harder to balance and the structures that defined our roles more rigid than we could have imagined. The education we had received was rock solid, but only a place to build from. Bob stuck around St. Bonaventure for another two years earning an MBA and coaching the soccer team before ultimately landing at General Electric. I was off to law school and then to the staff of the corporate legal department at IBM. Bob and I stayed in touch, usually comparing notes by telephone but occasionally finding opportunities to meet over a beer or two; as always seeing the world through different lenses but making surprisingly similar observations of the corporate environments we inhabited.

Four Loop Learning: The Art of Journaling and Reflective Leadership

Somewhere in that long-ago time, Bob showed me a journal he'd begun keeping. It was filled with ideas, flow charts, lists and quotes, but also self-criticisms and a few of those brilliant insights that we all have after the meetings are over, too late to be of value. Or were they? It was easy to see that Bob was on to something – that there was value to be harvested from those after-the-fact bits of hallway wisdom and also recognition of something profound: we are the masters of our own personal/professional growth in the organizations we serve. While the best run organizations spend considerable effort creating programs that help their people grow, each of us has the opportunity to make a decision: we can choose to be passive participants in those programs, accepting the lessons they offer but without a commitment to our own growth, or we can reach out and embrace not just the formal lessons such programs provide, but also the growth opportunities that lie between the lines of our daily lives.

Over the years Bob refined the journaling process as the pile of journals in his office grew high. Eventually the collected wisdom in those chronicles warranted two long shelves of their own, with another volume always in the works and close at hand. The reality is that nearly all of us spend so much of our energy addressing the tasks associated with our jobs and our personal lives that we never take the time to reflect on our experiences, good and bad, to capture the value of our own best ideas or to truly observe and learn from the people we work with. Corporate leadership development programs can be great, but there are lessons close at hand that can contribute to our growth as leaders. While Bob Cancalosi's journaling program is ambitious, (and perhaps even a bit daunting at first) its end design is to make you a better, more effective and efficient leader. The real secret of the journaling is in the discipline it creates. Instead of reacting to problems and seemingly endless crises, journaling creates the space to learn from where we've been and then to anticipate what will likely follow. That capacity – to be able to anticipate and then to plan and act in an intelligent and timely fashion is what separates exceptional managers from merely good ones. It reduces team stress while promoting better and more consistent results. And that is why exceptional managers get paid the big bucks – because they are worth it.

It's also probably safer than paddling around on a flood stage river in the middle of the night.

Joel and I enjoying the outdoors, with no canoe in sight.

MY JOURNEY INTO FOUR LOOP LEARNING

In December of 2017, my family and I toasted a great year. I was surrounded by my loved ones, the joy of the holiday season was upon us, I just completed a terrific 31-year career at GE, and, physically, I felt pretty terrific. In short, I was completely unaware of the medical odyssey upon which I was about to embark.

One week later, the right side of my face was completely paralyzed.

A very rare cancer was detected, growing on my facial nerve and invading the nerve's function. I suddenly had a right eye that would not blink, a right nostril that would not flare, and a smile that drooped to a frown on the right side — all scary!

In these types of medical challenges, you have no real choice but to learn to act quickly, find the best possible medical care with the most experienced doctors, and then just lean into adversity with the goal of *you defining it* versus *it defining you*.

The ensuing journey was long and complicated. I'll share one aspect of it here, because it shows how the art of journaling, which I have been practicing for over 20 years, really helped me get through a very challenging time.

> "GOING THROUGH THINGS YOU NEVER THOUGHT YOU WOULD GO THROUGH WILL ONLY TAKE YOU TO PLACES YOU NEVER THOUGHT YOU WOULD GET TO."
>
> — MORGAN HARPER NICHOLS

When I started journaling a couple decades ago, I created a process of Recording, Reflecting, Acting, and Sharing my experiences — what I began to refer to as "Four Loops." I decided to use this process to make a record of my entire medical experience on a daily basis as I completed thirty-three Proton Beam radiation and five Chemotherapy treatments over a two-month period.

In this context, "Record" means taking careful notes. I wrote about every memorable conversation and observation that I could from the long line of personal and professional caregivers that helped me to address the cancer and travel down the path of the unknown.

> "Hardships often prepare ordinary people for an extraordinary destiny"
> - C.S. Lewis

To capture all of those conversations — from the diagnosis, to discussion of the myriad treatment options, to explanations of complications that sometimes followed and the many milestones along the way — I recorded notes about every appointment, question and discussion into a journal. This proved to be an extremely practical and useful habit, to say the least. Daily recording provided a treasure of valuable information and medical insights which helped guide my wife and I to make the best, most informed decisions we could.

Think, for a moment, of the emotional turmoil that invades when your doctor starts saying things like *cancer* and *surgery* and *radiation* and *chemotherapy.* Making a contemporaneous, written record of those conversations created a reference point and continuity that allowed me to return to the information when I had questions, to do my own research, to continue the conversation with the next doctor and even with the same doctor days later.

Perhaps less obvious, but equally important, the process of recording kept me grounded in the moment. By making the conscious decision to capture all of that information, I was making the *unconscious* commitment to be a full participant in my own care and wellness.

I am human and yes, there were moments when my mind wandered into the land of "what-if's" and "why." The presence of the notebook and pen in my hand, however, were cues that I needed to be focused on the "here, now." By journaling through these events, I maintained a sense that I had some control over the process in a time of worry. That was empowering.

In the meantime, in addition to my written journal, I kept an online blog so that friends and family could follow along as I journeyed through treatment, surgery, more treatment, and more surgery. It was a new experience for me and a helpful distraction as it facilitated interaction with friends via comments.

It took some time before I could reflect on what I had written due to the intensity of the physical experience, which included multiple surgeries and a lengthy hospitalization. After reviewing my notes, I saw that I had learned so much from this and needed to share the key lessons with the important people in my life.

This overview allowed me to categorize the lessons into an alignment of **Head** (how I thought about things), **Heart** (how I felt or inspired others), and **Hand** (what I did). Consistent journaling and regular reflection enabled me to come up quite quickly with these lessons; I'd journaled every day and had lots of material.

One of the great things about a consistent journaling methodology is that it provides a vehicle for *synthesizing* the insights, wisdom, and experiences of those with whom we interact. My journaling practice goes back over twenty years and now includes more than 68 volumes. Those volumes include my own thoughts, but also those of the executives I was honored to work with at GE and those of the many customers that I was privileged to work with at the GE management university at Crotonville, New York. While I have always gone through the process of recording, reflecting, acting, and sharing the content from my journals, I began a practice of regularly going back through those many volumes. That's where *synthesis* occurs — combining those retrieved insights with new ideas to formulate broader understanding and powerful lessons.

Four Loop Learning: The Art of Journaling and Reflective Leadership

That method helped me to compile the list of fifteen life lessons that appears on page 25. I've been privileged to share these lessons with people in my network and the further benefit of their input in refining the list.

In my medical journey you can really see the four loops in action:

1. **RECORD -** the daily record of my medical experience.
2. **REFLECT -** deep reflection on the experience and lessons from personal interactions and curiosity which generated the 15 life lessons.
3. **ACT -** how I made life and attitude changes based upon regular reflections (especially "Cut People Slack," because you cannot know the burdens that people quietly carry).
4. **SHARE -** share the 15 lessons with people in my personal and professional network.

The "Sharing" loop drove me to write this book. I've learned by observing that the most effective leaders are "Servant Leaders," and that they freely share their knowledge with others to help them fulfill their ambitions and act more powerfully to live successful lives. Sharing has helped me become a much better leader, and the unselfish approach of giving to others to help them fulfill their ambitions is the motivation behind this book.

This was reinforced when I saw this quote on the check-in desk for Chemotherapy:

> "Be fearless in the pursuit of what sets your soul on fire"
> ~Anonymous

It is based upon this principle and how it personally set my soul on fire that I'd like to share what I've learned about journaling with you.

So, "Let me share something with you."

15 SIGNIFICANT LIFE LESSONS TO SHARE FROM MY MEDICAL JOURNEY

HEAD - how you think

1. Positivity and humor accelerate the healing
2. Look for the silver linings as they are in abundance and hidden in the smallest of places
3. Keep your eye on the prize, which is short term healing for long term health
4. If adversity unexpectedly hits you, it's better for you to define it versus letting it define you
5. Go in with a positive headset and be resilient

HAND - what you do

6. Cut people slack as we don't know the hidden burdens that people quietly carry
7. Early detection is key, and then seeking experienced doctors is an advantage
8. Let others help you as it also really helps them
9. Don't forget the power of sharing your story with others
10. Recognize great service and thank them to reinforce it

HEART - how you feel or inspire others

11. Enormously love your caregivers
12. Be grateful every day and really value the power of prayer and meditation
13. Life is precious and short, so live every day to the fullest and take nothing for granted
14. Appreciate what you have in life right now
15. Hope for the best, but also mentally prepare for the long haul

THE ACT OF SHARING

The first question is, "Why is sharing so valuable?"

Many of the most transformative leadership discussions begin with a simple phrase: "Let me share something with you." It might be said by a manager seeking to offer perspective to one of her employees, or she might use the phrase to bring a persistent challenge to her mentor as she seeks advice. The beauty of "let me share" is that it doesn't matter who uses it to start the conversation.

The act of "sharing" is immensely powerful. Unlike "telling" or "instructing," sharing carries with it an acknowledgment: it's less about the thing you want to say and more about the person being addressed. You are, in effect, asking for their partnership. In that moment, you are letting the other person see a different side of you, thus bringing more of your whole, authentic self to the discussion.

"Let me share" implies a willingness to be vulnerable: you're not pretending you have the answer, or that you've fully framed the problem. You're simply offering what you hope is a helpful perspective. It's a far cry from saying: "Here's what you should do!" And, it shows empathy, by clearly signaling that you want to take a break from the frenetic flow of life to connect more deeply with a fellow human being.

I have made a career of studying leadership, which has included keeping journals to capture the best thinking of the leaders and co-workers who influenced my own growth. In addition to the ideas

> "WE MAKE A LIVING BY WHAT WE GET, BUT WE MAKE A LIFE BY WHAT WE GIVE."
>
> — WINSTON CHURCHILL

and inspiration they shared with me, I kept track of my own reflections and insights.

Over the course of that journey, I quickly learned that I needed more than a notebook and a pen. I needed a process. I needed a way to not merely jot down those ideas, but to organize them in a way that would allow the knowledge to build and grow over time.

In this book, I share the secrets of my journaling and take you through the steps of beginning your own journaling process.

What I've created and refined is a reflective learning process comprised of four interconnected components of **Recording**, **Reflecting**, **Acting**, and **Sharing**. I refer to these components as the **Four Loops of Learning**.

The lessons from the journals and the Four Loop Learning process have a relevant connection to the following Chinese proverb:

"Give a man a fish and feed him for a day,
Teach a man to fish and you feed him for a lifetime"

It might be said that sharing the contents of 68 journals compiled from over twenty years of daily journaling and hundreds of leadership lessons is "giving a fish," but sharing the Four Loop Process is my way of "teaching you to fish." Journaling is a simple method for capturing, refining, and harvesting your own best ideas. By committing to the process, you'll build a personal treasure chest of reflective thoughts, best practices, and leadership ideas.

Four Loop Learning has been immensely valuable to me and, I hope, to those around me. Let's face it — we have many facets of our professional and personal lives to keep track of, and relying on short term memory and intuition to address important matters is a losing game. The day-to-day demands of our jobs easily grab our attention, and instances where we can actually reach our desk before being confronted with the first

> "When you learn, teach. When you get, give."
> - Maya Angelou

The Act of Sharing

challenge of the morning are few and far between. As business cycles are compressed and the complexity of the world increases, those opportunities are becoming even rarer.

With such tough demands, how do we find room to grow as managers and as leaders? For that matter, how do we find time to ensure that our personal health is being attended to with the same regularity and vigilance as, for example, our latest project? The answer to these important questions is that we need a process that allows us the luxury of remembering where we've been as well as the gift of developing our own best ideas into usable tools.

My own process...

Since 1985, I have served in multiple leadership and general management roles at General Electric, an organization known for managerial excellence and for courageously reinventing itself several times in its 125-year history. My career path has included positions in GE's Silicones, Plastics, Healthcare, and Corporate Divisions, and eight years as the Chief Learning Officer for GE Healthcare. Most recently I was honored to serve as Director of Customer Leadership Education at GE's prestigious global learning institute, The Jack Welch Leadership Center, also known as "Crotonville" for its location in bucolic Westchester County, New York. Founded in 1956 as the first corporate university, Crotonville is where some of the world's top managers and political figures have honed their leadership skills. It shouldn't surprise you to read that the learning experiences in this rarefied air flowed in both directions.

At Crotonville, I was privileged to lead a team that delivered about 100 leadership programs each year to more than 5,000 senior leaders from GE's customer organizations around the world. In addition to working with so many talented GE employees, I was exposed to many truly brilliant people whose skills and experiences literally spanned the globe.

The GE team's mission in developing and presenting custom tailored programs was to help those organizations identify the problems that were holding their organizations back, leverage the talent they already possessed, and begin the process of developing solutions that allowed them to move forward with greater purpose and results.

In that process I learned that most companies declare that their challenges are unique to their culture and their environment, yet I found that everyone really has the same kinds of issues to solve — such as finding and developing great talent, inspiring their workforce, and getting employees aligned on the mission, vision, and purpose statements that are supposed to drive corporate action. Having come to the realization that most organizations struggled with the same issues and also seeing that their leaders were truly talented people, I began to wonder why those managers hadn't been able to articulate solutions without outside assistance.

Some of the early years' journals.

It took some time, but eventually I realized that for many of those talented managers, the real problem was that they lacked a disciplined process for reflection — they were so busy putting out fires that they were unable to capture and take advantage of their own best ideas. Though I'd always journaled for my own benefit, it occurred to me that there was value in the process for others.

Throughout my career I've led several company-wide initiatives in quality management, cultural transformation, and leadership development. Those experiences taught me much about the art of leadership and change management. I've also been a regular speaker at Harvard's Advanced Management Program and at Northwestern University's Kellogg School of Management. Speaking at those revered institutions is humbling! The students represent the best and brightest of rising management talent from around the globe. Hardly an hour goes past without someone advancing an idea that challenges the assumptions that form the foundation of my understanding of people and the organizations they inhabit. And, in turn, those lessons inform my world view and help me to prepare keynote addresses on leadership and learning for organizations like Ted-X, Business Innovation Forum, and CLO conferences.

So, here's the punch line: I believe that I learn more from these individuals than they learn from me.

With so many great ideas flowing from these brilliant minds, the challenge has always been in capturing and synthesizing the concepts into managerial lessons that helped me become a better leader. The paradigms from my education and experiences that seemed to have been locked in stone for decades were being deeply contested — these learning opportunities opened a whole new aperture on how to think differently about things. The late C.K. Prahalad called this "dominant logic," referring to our deeply held assumptions about the world. Journaling is an effective way to keep on poking at those deeply held assumptions and find more relevant interpretations. Over the years I've learned that all interpretations are valid, but not all interpretations are of equal value. Journaling keeps me on the constant pursuit of finding a higher value.

Luckily, I took good notes!

In just over 20 years, I have filled 68 journals with the experiences and insights I've gained. Those journals have served me well at GE in teaching and reinforcing leadership best practices. They have also become a valuable personal touchpoint that help me focus on the most important things in life.

The habits I've developed through journaling have made it possible to maintain a healthy work-life balance in a world where it has become harder and harder to excel at one without cost to the other. These habits also provided me with a platform to see things and build on them as my experiences and learnings expanded over time. I've learned to utilize the lessons from the journal contents — I've always liked the quote, "Content is king, and context is the kingdom."

Initially, I thought that a major focus on providing deeper context would help leaders accelerate their impact. However, the reflective learnings from years of journaling have allowed me to add a bit more perspective to this quote by adapting it with the following extension, which I call the 5 C's:

> "Content is king, and context is the kingdom, while connecting the dots to what the customers value and collaborating across your organization is the universe."

It's putting the content and context into action that is aligned to what your customers value — and then ensuring that the resources in your organization are efficiently aligned and working together in a collaborative way to generate a bigger impact with longer-term satisfaction. This adaptation helps me assess the quotes I record, informing what could be added to provide deeper meaning.

It was with that in mind that, after years of sharing Four Loop Learning techniques with individuals and small groups, I committed

The Act of Sharing

to sharing more widely via my first book. My hope is that it will be helpful to you in your own personal and professional leadership journey.

We'll start with a look at journaling in general, and then I'll explain in detail the Four Loops of Learning. Finally, I'll guide you through setting up your journal and its various components and tools.

So, let's start fishing!

WHAT IS JOURNALING?

People who have little or no experience with journaling often assume it to be similar to writing in a diary — at the end of the day, a soulful practitioner cracks open a blank book and starts with the words, "Dear Diary, here's what happened today…"

The sort of journaling that we're going to explore in this book is actually related to a practice from the 17th century called "commonplacing." In those days, people with literary and/or intellectual ambitions maintained a "commonplace book." In its simplest form, it was a place to transcribe particularly inspirational, provocative, or useful textual passages from one's reading.

For many poets and writers, the physical act of transcribing material from a profound or inspirational writer was a way of "absorbing" some of the writer's skills. Intellectuals like Sir Francis Bacon, John Locke, and John Milton swore by this method for enhancing their memories and widening their mental scope. They recorded in their commonplace books overheard conversations, observations, found facts, and anything else gathered during the course of a day.

The real value of commonplacing went beyond merely archiving interesting material. Through regular reviews of the entries in the books, disparate ideas and notions were suddenly viewed in proximity to one another, creating new insights and, as we described earlier, "synthesis."

"A BLANK SPACE IS NO EMPTY SPACE. IT IS BRIMMING WITH POTENTIAL. IT IS A MASTERPIECE IN WAITING —YOURS."

A. A. PATAWARAN

Four Loop Learning: The Art of Journaling and Reflective Leadership

Author Steven Johnson uses the phrase "idea remixes." He studied the philosopher John Locke's approach to commonplacing as published in 1652, and, during a lecture at Columbia University, related Locke's "instruction for use" as expressed in his canonical work An Essay Concerning Human Understanding:

> When I meet with any thing, that I think fit to put into my common-place-book, I first find a proper head. Suppose, for example that the head be EPISTOLA, I look unto the index for the first letter and the following vowel which in this instance are E I, if in the space marked E I there is a number that directs me to the page designed for words that begin with an E and whose first vowel, after the initial letter, is I, I must then write under the word EPISTOLA in that page, what I have to remark.

Locke's approach seems almost comical in its intricacy, but it was a response to a specific set of design constraints: creating a functional index in only two pages that could be expanded as the book accumulated more quotes and observations. In a certain sense, this is a search algorithm, a defined series of steps that allows the user to index the text in a way that makes it easier to query.

For years now, we of the "digital generation" have experienced something very loosely related to Locke's indexing system every time we do a Google search. Even so, a valuable "serendipitous discovery" is much more likely to occur in a physical format, particularly one that is handwritten and maintained by you — whether by a system complicated as Locke's, or simple as my Four Loop method.

> "He listens well who takes notes."
> - Dante Alighieri

There is also the added value found in the physical process of handwriting. It isolates and sharpens focus because you really can't multitask when you are writing by hand. If you type on a computer, it's much easier to get distracted by e-mails and pop-ups on a screen that basically invites regular "taps of the shoulder" from outside of your zone of concentration.

MY JOURNALING ORIGINS

When I started journaling twenty years ago, I didn't know what a commonplace book was. I did know, however, that I was in a terrific learning environment at GE and wanted to be able to collect and recall as much information and as many lessons as possible.

Journaling has always been intriguing to me. As a child, Da Vinci's *Codex Leicester* was transfixing, and I tried in vain to draw the things I saw on its pages. Later I would pause my *Raiders of the Lost Ark* videotape to get a closer look at Indiana Jones' adventure and exploration journal. He had maps and diagrams and intricate notes in there, and I strained my eyes on an analog screen to see what secrets would reveal themselves.

My journaling efforts intensified after I read *Outliers* by Malcolm Gladwell, wherein he famously posited that to be exceptional at anything, 10,000 hours of practice is required. So, I thought, if I string out 10,000 hours over ten years, that equates to 2.7 hours per day of practice and attention over the course of each year. Following Gladwell's advice seemed like a good guideline for becoming a great professional development leader for GE. I was quite humbled when I read an article in *Business Week* revealing that professional golfer Tiger Woods achieved 10,000 hours of golf practice by age twelve.

> "Success is nothing more than a few simple disciplines practiced every day."
> - Jim Rohn

But even if my time commitment was significant and well-focused, I needed more. Specifically, I needed a framework for recording everything I was learning in an accessible format.

Reviewing Journal 29 in 2014, Oconomowoc, WI.

Consistent journaling became my core method of applying daily attention to what I'd learned, or needed to learn, as well as a dependable way to track items of significance in all areas of my life. It was and is a scheduled island of focus that greatly eased and, eventually, eliminated my anxiety regarding "herding information."

I also learned that **teaching material to others** is when you are really tested as to how much you really know about a particular topic, and the act of instruction strengthens your grasp of the material. Any opportunity to pass along knowledge is of benefit to both the teacher and student!

Most importantly, the journaling method had to be **relatively easy to maintain and incredibly useful day to day**. It is this last point – incredibly useful day to day – that drove the process that evolved into the Four Loops.

What is Journaling?

INTO THE LOOPS

Learning theorists tell us that, while there are many individual learning styles, we all internalize, synthesize, and build on existing knowledge when we can reliably reflect on our ongoing impressions. It helps enormously to record those impressions by distilling experiences into a few thoughts and putting them to paper.

Going further, if we can access and synthesize those experiences and observations to make them ingredients in a repertoire of skills to apply as managers, we grow and help our teams and organizations reach their goals. The highest application of these lessons occurs, of course, when we teach them to others.

This is the essence of Four Loop Learning:

- **RECORDING distilled thoughts and observations**
- **REFLECTING on lessons and ultimately determining your "Best in Journal," which is your most significant learning in each journal**
- **ACTING on your most significant learning**
- **SHARING those lessons with others to help them be better leaders, and also deepen your own understanding by teaching**

BENEFITS OF JOURNALING

The process of recording, reflecting, acting, and sharing has helped me become a better leader in the following ways:

- Deliberate reflection allows me to slow down and think about things in a deeper context with more viewpoints. Once a proposed action was more thoroughly reviewed, its implementation was actually faster and more efficient.

- It shows people you really care when you take the time to record the relevant points of your conversation with them and then check back for understanding.

- Journaling provides a record of my thoughts, feelings, ideas, and points of view at a specific point in time. It's been extremely valuable to look back at my cognitive starting points and see how much my perspective has grown over time.

- It's an effective way to create an initial idea or model and then iterate and watch the progression build over time.

- I find it very therapeutic to write things down and then forget about them knowing they are safely stored in a journal which I can find at a later point in time.

THE BENEFITS OF JOURNALING

Many professionals are familiar with and swear by the Getting Things Done (GTD) method as made popular by David Allen. Count me among those who flew through his book, highlighter in hand and nodding regularly. The basic philosophy of "GTD" is very simple: the mind is for ideas, not for storing information. GTD presents a series of steps for regularly "offloading" and reviewing myriad data items, ideas, to-do lists, priorities, and goals. Once a trusted system and routine for storing and reviewing your life's information is in place, your mind no longer has to waste wavelength or capacity on recall and anxiety about whether or not proper attention is being paid to each and every facet of life.

THE NEED FOR BETTER LEARNING HABITS

Charles Duhigg wrote an excellent book called *The Power of Habit*, and in it he explores how we create habits — good and bad — as well as methods of creating "automatic behaviors" that make it possible to regularly accomplish great things.

> "A mind that is stretched by a new experience can never go back to its old dimensions."
> - Oliver Wendell Holmes

Four Loop Learning leverages the power of "habit loops" to maintain focus and reward engagement. After just a few experiences of having information, people, and ideas at your fingertips as needed, you will require very little prompting to make time for journaling every single day. And, as you dedicate time to daily reflection, you will be able to think more deeply without distraction.

In Cal Newport's book, *Deep Work*, he cites research showing that the average worker spends 60% of their work week engaged in electronic communications and internet searching. He also found that 30% of a worker's time is dedicated to reading and answering e-mail.

Reflective journaling allows you to be in a distraction-free concentration zone, so you can achieve what Newport refers to as the ideal environment to push your cognitive capabilities to the limit.

THE POWER OF PURPOSE

Journaling can also help you detect, define, and refine your purpose. I'm often reminded of the following quote from Travis Bradberry and Jean Graves of *Emotional Intelligence 2.0* on how powerful a purpose-driven culture can be:

> "People will work hard for a paycheck, even harder for a person, but they will work hardest for a purpose."

In a July/Aug 2018 *Harvard Business Review* article entitled "When Work Has Meaning," authors Robert E. Quinn & Anjan V. Thaker shared research revealing that connecting people to a higher sense of purpose can inspire them and bring more energy and creativity to their jobs. Journaling is therapeutic and diagnostic in that it allows us to connect actions to purpose, in real time.

The act of regular journaling conditions us to be better listeners and more aware of our surroundings. It enhances our curiosity and prompts us to ask more probing questions. It also helps us to see how our thinking changes as our knowledge and capabilities grow. I've learned many things by "connecting the dots" within and between journals. (The Ambition Flowchart, described later in this book, is one such example that will be explained in the Record Loop.)

Clearly, for persons searching for purpose and its demonstrated benefits, journaling is a vital tool.

UNCOVERING BLIND SPOTS

The Johari Window, created by the psychologist team of Joseph Left and Harrington Ingham in 1955, is a technique that helps people understand their relationships with themselves and others in terms

What is Journaling?

of what is seen from different perspectives. Journaling can help us access that dark spot in our Johari Window: the side of us that others see, but which remain hidden from us.

By recording outcomes that disappoint us — professional relationships which have faltered, goals we didn't achieve — we more fully and honestly process these events, and, over time, you will note that patterns emerge. Though it may require further discussion with a trusted party to truly understand our weaknesses and vulnerabilities, the act of journaling can enhance and accelerate the improvements we choose to make. Great learning can occur when we realize our failures and faults and proactively make changes to become more effective.

JOHARI WINDOW

	KNOWN TO SELF	NOT KNOWN TO SELF
KNOWN TO OTHERS	KNOWN SELF: THINGS WE KNOW ABOUT OURSELVES AND OTHERS KNOW ABOUT US	BLIND SELF: THINGS OTHERS KNOW ABOUT US THAT WE DO NOT KNOW
NOT KNOWN TO OTHERS	HIDDEN SELF: THINGS WE KNOW ABOUT OURSELVES THAT OTHERS DO NOT KNOW	UNKNOWN SELF: THINGS NEITHER WE NOR OTHERS KNOW ABOUT US

> "Men succeed when they realize their failures are their preparations for victories."
> - Ralph Waldo Emerson

I also find that my ability to share information and create mentoring and development opportunities for others is enormously enhanced by journaling. By noting and regularly reviewing the needs and goals of my colleagues, and mapping to my own experiences and reflection points, I am free to become an asset for others.

In a July 2017 *Harvard Business* article, Dan Ciampa shared his insights into why he kept a journal when he was a CEO. Ciampa observed strong evidence that writing reinforces learning as it provides a process to deliberately slow down and use the benefit of time intervals to generate better solutions.

Dan described his experience with a technique called the "Second Solution Method" where, after a round of brainstorming, you take a break, do something else, and then come back with another round of brainstorming. The benefit of time intervals resulted in more robust and innovative ideas that led to higher impact solutions and results during his tenure as CEO.

> "The illiterate of the 21st century will not be those who cannot read, but those who cannot learn, unlearn, and relearn."
> - Alvin Toffler

Dan's observation was also supported by the research of Dr. Scott Isaksen in his book *Creative Approaches to Problem Solving*. He referred to the same benefit as "Extended Effort Principle," and Scott's research shows that breakthrough and novel ideas come from purposely doing a few more rounds of brainstorming after taking deliberate breaks.

After learning from both of these experts, I started adding in a "time out" to the brainstorming sessions I led and found the quality and quantity of ideas to be so much more valuable, with much deeper linkages to addressing challenges.

JOURNALING DEFINED

I use the word journaling as an all-encompassing term to record things in life that are meaningful and relevant to me.

From my perspective, journaling includes the recording of:

- Ideas
- Models
- Observations
- Best practices
- Quotes
- Excerpts
- Connection points
- Articles
- TED Talks
- Bucket List activation reminders
- Trackers
- Drawings/sketches
- Trends detected
- Strategic planning
- Important to-do lists
- Podcasts
- YouTube Videos

And so much more! The components of what you can journal are endless and limited only by you.

"Executives are constrained not by resources but by their imaginations"
~ C.K. Prahalad

What is Journaling?

My journaling has evolved over time. I initially started journaling a few times throughout the day in five- to ten-minute increments when some aspect of learning deeply resonated with me and set off my curiosity antennae, which made me want to record it before I lost it.

My daily time investment in journaling has dramatically crept up over the years as I reaped the rewards of regular recording. My current routine is to journal approximately 30 minutes every morning when I wake up, with a cup of hot brewed coffee. I start by noting what I'm grateful for, followed by whatever big leadership thoughts are on my mind. I continue with a few hours throughout the day in multiple sessions as ideas and thoughts come to me, finishing with about 30 minutes at night. It's amazing how quickly I transitioned from ten to twenty minutes to almost three hours every day after two decades. I find tranquility in writing things down, especially at night — it helps me sleep better.

> "I'm not a teacher, but an awakener."
> - Robert Frost

If you're like me and frequently travel on business, just about every flight presents a quiet opportunity to review and reflect upon our recordings. I'm always thinking deeply about where I am spending my time and the types of thoughts that are dominating my mental billboard space as recorded in the journals. I also like to look at where I'm spending my energy and assess whether it's aligned to my ambition. All in all, it meets Malcolm Gladwell's "2.7 hours per day" guideline, and after having practiced this routine for twenty years, the time devoted to reflection and planning has been immeasurably valuable.

> "I don't divide the world into the weak or the strong or the successes or failures ... I divide the world into learners and non-learners."
> - Benjamin Barber

I believe that the most important decision a leader makes every day is where they invest their time. We all have the same 1440 minutes in our day, and I'm constantly observing why some people get so much done and others so little.

As Peter Drucker stated:

> "One half of the leaders I work with have to figure out what they need to stop doing"

Deliberate journaling can provide you with the time-outs to reflect on your approach and help you better determine things you should seriously consider stopping. As managers, leaders, and family members, the decisions we make about allocating that most precious resource can have an enormous impact on our own quality of life and the quality of the relationships we have with others.

KEYBOARD VS. HANDWRITING

I am often asked why I handwrite the journals, especially in a "digital world." The reason is quite simple: you retain more learning when you physically hand-write, versus tapping out words on a keyboard.

I learned from Scott Halford's book, *Activate the Brain*, that we create better memory trails in the brain when we physically write the words down versus typing them into a device. His assertion that handwriting is like "strength training for the brain" reinforced my desire to journal even more.

Modern college lecture halls are filled with students tapping away on laptops, and often these students can actually input notes quicker via keyboard than by handwriting. However, research by Pam Mueller and David Oppenheimer from their work published in *Psychological Science* shows certain advantages when notes are written out by hand.

In three experiments, Mueller and Oppenheimer had students take notes in a classroom setting. Afterward, they tested them. Half of the group were told to take notes on a laptop and the other group were told to take handwritten notes.

Confirming the conclusions reached in other studies, the students with laptops consistently took more notes — clearly, they

What is Journaling?

win the quantity argument. However, those who wrote out their notes by hand had a stronger conceptual understanding of what they had heard and were more successful

> "To do two things at once is to do neither."
> - Publilius Syrus

in applying and integrating the material than the laptop-users. In fact, hand-writers scored twice as well as the keyboarders on tests following the lectures.

The scientists doubted their findings at first, thinking that perhaps the hand-writers had simply spent more time studying before the tests. They tried the experiment again, this time taking away both groups' notes immediately following the lecture. A week later, they tested the entire combined group and found the hand writers still performed better.

Mueller and Oppenheimer believe that writing out information by hand requires a different sort of cognitive processing than typing. Because of the speed with many keyboard-savvy students can type (Generation X and Millennials grew up prowling the QWERTY keypad landscape) they basically *transcribe* what they hear rather than *processing* the material in a way that handwriting requires.

Persons who wrote by hand had to conceptualize the material in order to make choices and keep up — which adds up to more mental heavy lifting than simple transcription. This is sometimes referred to as "creating disfluency," which relies on a bit of work for the mind in terms of sorting, choice-making, categorizing and physically encoding (writing) at the time of acquisition.

Even when keyboard users were warned to avoid transcribing what they heard and instead summarized material in their own words, students with laptops could not stop themselves from verbatim, "low impact" rote repetition of the material presented.

In his book *The Shallows*, author Nicholas Carr expresses the relationship between human beings and tools:

When a carpenter takes his hammer into his hand, he can use that hand to do only what that hammer can do. The hand becomes an implement for pounding and pulling nails. When a soldier put the binoculars to his eyes, he can only see what the lenses allow him to see. His field of view lengthens but becomes blind to what is nearby. Nietzsche's experience with his typewriter provides a particularly good illustration of the way technologies exert their influence on us. Not only did the philosopher come to imagine that his writing ball was "a thing like me"; he also sensed that he was becoming a thing like it, that his typewriter was shaping his thoughts.

> "When you have to use more energy to put those words down, you are more apt to make them count."
> - Raymond Chandler

As enormously helpful as computing devices and keyboard entry are in our day-to-day lives — professional and otherwise — it cannot be denied that they are tools like any other. Their usage can and will alter how and what we express, as well as our pattern of thought while recording information. So, while there is certainly a great deal of value in digital note taking — copy-and-paste rearranging, search capabilities, accessibility across multiple devices in multiple locations, quick voice input — my preference for journaling remains ink-on-paper and physical notebooks.

Think of your journal and your writing time as a place separated from the keyboarding you do the rest of the day. The pace is different and helps establish a new "mind space" for your set-aside period. Also, you can't multitask when you are journaling.

Writing by hand may feel uncomfortable at first. You may look at your "chicken scratch" and wrinkle your nose. Don't let that stop you! After a few weeks of practice, you will begin to slow yourself down — part of the benefit of handwriting — and see improvement in your penmanship.

What is Journaling?

Meanwhile, the "disfluency" created by having to get words on paper in a legible manner will go a long way toward avoiding "informational blindness." In a recent *New York Times* Article, Dr. Susan Dynarski, a professor at the University of Michigan, says she bans electronics in the classroom because of the distraction impact she calls "visual pollution." Her research shows that laptops distract us from learning, both for the user and for those around them. Her study has also been supported with research at Princeton, UCLA and the US Military Academy. Dr. Dynarski uses an economic term to describe the impact called "negative externality," and associates the distraction from electronics as a form of "second-hand smoke."

Handwritten journaling avoids this distraction and allows you to focus on what you are learning.

And don'y worrey about mispelings or making misteakes as it's the thought that counts, not the spelling or penmanship.

THE FOUR LOOPS OF LEARNING

There are dozens of learning models, and educators will debate different approaches among themselves until the end of time. It will come as no surprise to learn that the element everyone can agree upon is that memory is a key factor in learning.

Memory is tricky. John J. Medina, a developmental molecular biologist and Director of the Brain Center for Applied Learning Research at Seattle Pacific University, flat out admits: "We really don't know how the brain keeps track of things."

He does, however, effectively explain some of the basic principles of memory. The most important rule in capturing short-term memory, he says, is **Repeat to Remember**. To convert these to long-term memory, he advises to **Remember to Repeat**.

The importance of reflection was also reinforced when I heard brain expert Nigel Paine share the five things we know about the brain when it comes to learning:

1. **Stress thwarts learning**
2. **Brains like multi-media stimulation**
3. **Brains like to learn together**
4. **More physical fitness helps the brain learn faster**
5. **Brains like to process and need time to synthesize and reflect**

> "WE ARE WHAT WE REPEATEDLY DO. EXCELLENCE THEN, IS NOT AN ACT, BUT A HABIT."
>
> — ARISTOTLE

Four Loop Learning: The Art of Journaling and Reflective Leadership

Journaling is my process of really investing in the power of deliberate reflection. I have learned that dedicated time to synthesize and reflect really helps me become a better leader by helping me slow down and think deeper to make better decisions — and ultimately go faster.

> "The great art of learning is to understand but little at a time."
> - John Locke

Many times the members of my network have asked me how to summarize the value of journaling. I share with them that **deliberate reflection for deeper inspection yields a higher impact direction.**

This brings us to the Four Loops of Learning that give my journaling method its name and help you make your information useful and mentally retrievable.

LOOP ONE: RECORDING OR NOTE TAKING

As you learned earlier, writing by hand has been shown to create better retention than capturing an audio recording or typing into a laptop. Scientists have found that the more elaborately we encode information at the moment of learning, the stronger the memory. The processing required to convert what we hear into summarized hand-written notes uses more mental horsepower than merely transcribing what we hear. Besides, the slower, more contemplative nature of writing by hand is conducive to mindfulness when collecting thoughts on paper.

> "We write twice to taste life twice, in the moment and in retrospect."
> - Anais Nin

LOOP TWO: REFLECTION

The Reflection Loop entails reviewing what you have recorded and then — surprise! — reflecting upon it. One of the most powerful habits in journaling is to regularly Stop & Reflect after every 50 pages you record to see what kinds of trends reveal themselves as you journal over time. The Stop & Reflect step is an opportunity to repeat information to better remember it, and the "every 50 pages" discipline enforces the "remember to repeat" dictum.

LOOP THREE: ACT

The Act Loop provides an opportunity for you to put your best reflective thoughts into action. This loop helps identify the most important thing you've learned in a specific journal — your Best in Journal — and further identify something that you are going to do differently as a result. In the learning metaphor of "What, So What, & Now What," this is the specific action that will answer the question, "Now, what are you going to do next?"

> "Act so that the maxim of your act could be made a principle of a universal law."
> - Immanuel Kant

LOOP FOUR: SHARE OR TEACH OTHERS

There is perhaps no better way to cement a concept to memory or master a methodology than to take the time to share and teach it to another person or persons.

I'm reminded of Aristotle's insight on learning:

> "Teaching is the purest form of learning."

For me, this is my favorite loop and the primary motivator for consistent journaling.

As you travel through the Four Loops regularly, you will find it easier and easier to retain, implement, and teach others the valuable lessons that present themselves to you every day.

> "Gratitude bestows many benefits. It dissolves negative feelings: anger and jealousy melt in its embrace, fear and defensiveness shrink. Gratitude deflated the barriers to love."
> - Roger Walsh

GETTING STARTED

Over the past decade, I have given out a few hundred journals. The biggest challenge the recipients express to me is that they don't know how to get started.

I've found that adding just a little bit of inspiration gets the ball rolling, and I tell people to try recording an exercise which I call "30 days of gratefulness." For 30 straight days, start the morning writing in your journal the things you are most grateful for that day! It makes the journaling easier and creates a positive beginning.

Then, after 30 days, review all 30 of your written reflections and see if you can detect any trends in what you wrote. This typically generates enough momentum to keep things going, as being grateful results in positive energy — and that's a great way to start the day.

A note on separating business and personal journaling: When I started journaling, I used to have specific notebooks for business and personal material. After a few months of carrying around two journals, I decided it was more efficient to utilize one journal for all aspects of my life. A simple marking system distinguishes between the two by classifying my recordings as either Personal or Professional.

LOOP 1: RECORD

One of the first things you will learn while journaling is that it is much more than writing things in a notebook. This is, after all, the art of note-taking.

When regular journaling becomes part of your day-to-day routine, you have introduced a meditative period to your life that did not previously exist. Journaling cannot occur while you are driving, or while you are on the phone with a colleague. It's virtually "multitask-proof" by the very nature of its physical requirements — a steady surface to write on and room to manipulate a pen.

This means you will seek out a time of day or place or places that allow for some level of quiet contemplation. Congratulations — you've scored a victory already, and you haven't even written a word.

> **"To chase two rabbits at once, you will catch neither."**
> **- Russian Proverb**

But let's get on to the writing anyway, shall we?

Record anything relevant — personal and professional — and use your Journal in sequence (i.e. don't skip pages). Later, in the chapter on Setting Up Your Journal, you'll learn about Legend categories. These are names to classify your learnings so it's easier to find them in future searches. As you write, you'll code your inputs to the Legend categories as they come up and create new ones that are relevant for you.

56

> "TONES SOUND, THEN ROAR AND STORM ABOUT ME UNTIL I HAVE SET THEM IN NOTES."
>
> LUDWIG VAN BEETHOVEN

Legend categories are great for helping you retrieve information of a certain sort without painstakingly having to read every word written. A box around the letter or symbol helps it stand out, and I generally fill it in with a highlighter as well.

Another way Legend categories are useful is in how they prompt you to record material inspired in part by those very categories. For instance, the fact that you know you have a category called "Q" for QUOTE will likely make you search your mind for something you heard today that is worth recording.

One example of using the Legend effectively occurs when I'm asked to create a leadership keynote on a specific topic. I peruse a few journals and look for some relevant quotes — clearly marked with a "Q" — to use as a compelling opening or to reinforce key points made throughout the presentation.

Here is an example of a quote I use when I want to reinforce how important it is for people to follow their dreams:

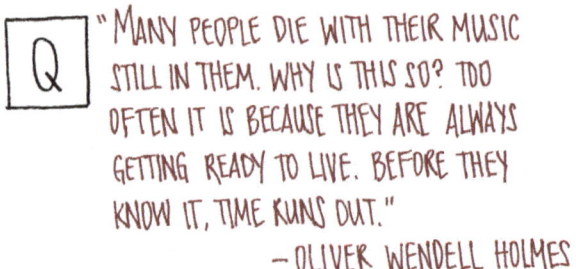

Some days you may fill up three, five, or even seven or more pages; other days could merit just a single page. The important thing is to make writing in your Journal a daily habit that you have to give very little thought to in terms of making time or space for the activity; it should become as habitual as brushing your teeth in the morning. After a while you'll feel the pull when it's time to write in your Journal, and there will be little or no need to consciously remember to do it.

> "Putting pen to paper lights more fires than matches ever will."
>
> - Malcolm Forbes

Other days, when I have absolutely nothing in me, I just write a few things that I'm thankful for. I find that this creates a good mood for the morning. I added a reminder page in the journal just in case I

Loop 1: Record

DID I CREATE A FIVE-MINUTE MEMORY TODAY?

Some of us think too much about the past; others obsess about the future. In both cases, we're missing out on the present — and we don't realize it until it's too late.

Focused and regular journaling allows us to address these imbalances. It enables us to put the past in perspective, and plan more clearly and intentionally for tomorrow. This, in turn, helps us to be more mindful in the moment and pay attention to what matters.

Mindfulness defined:

> *"Paying attention in a particular way: on purpose, in the present moment and non-judgmentally"*
>
> ~ Jon Kabat-Zinn, Center for Mindfulness

In my case, I was thinking too much about the future. It got to a point where the people I was with felt that I was disinterested — which wasn't true! I was not disinterested, I was *distracted* — by my own wide-ranging, future-focused thoughts. I had trouble remembering conversations because too much of my mind was elsewhere. So, I decided to create a learning intervention for myself. My goal was to free up sufficient mental capacity to remember not just a comment or an image, but a continuous, high-definition track of my own life.

For example, when I'm on family vacation, I purposely try to find as many five-minute memories as possible. If it's a conversation, I try to remember not just a snippet, but the whole thing — the way people looked, the way they were feeling, the atmosphere.

If it's a photo being taken, I don't just recall the second the shutter snaps, I try to remember everything that happened before and after. I try to remember anything and everything that makes my heart glow. The more present I am in the moment, the richer my five-minute memory. And if I'm really lucky — and really present — the memory is even longer and more vivid.

We're all moving too fast. Journaling helps us to slow down the world, build mental capacity, be more present in each moment, and live our purpose. It allows me to reflect on these kinds of questions:

- **What did I say?**
- **What did I do?**
- **What did I learn?**
- **How do I need to think and act differently to accelerate the path towards my ambition?**
- **What can I do tomorrow to function best as a leader and friend?**
- **And, if I made a mistake what can I learn from it?**

My friend Rich Ruhman from the US Air Force said that "just because you make a mistake does not mean you are one." Record them and reflect!

JOURNAL REFLECTION

What a great day to pause for a moment and count your blessings.

What are 5 things you are really grateful for in your life right now?

1. _____

2. _____

3. _____

4. _____

5. _____

get too bogged down in things that are not as important. (See an example of the Journal Reflection layout on the opposite page.)

Every now and then you'll note something that you're *sure* you'll need to retrieve or consult in the near future. This is where you deploy a tab from your inside-front-cover tab inventory, making that material easy to find. Perhaps it's a group of notes related to a pending meeting or travel information for an upcoming trip. Sometimes you'll mark material that you anticipate will be included in the Stop & Reflect.

The bottom line is to get your thoughts, ideas, plans, observations, etc. on paper in a trusted collection device so you mind can be freed from mundane storage functions and instead generate more ideas.

FOUR EXAMPLES OF LOOP ONE JOURNALING ACTIVITIES

I. AMBITION FLOWCHART

My focus on the ambition flowchart really started when I came across the following quote from Mark Twain:

> **"Let the beauty of what you love be what you do."**
> **- Rumi**

> "The two most important days in your life are the day you are born and the day you figure out why."

This quote triggered multiple questions in me, my family, and good friends on how to better define our respective "WHY" and really understand what we are individually passionate about. Doing what we love results in greater joy and job satisfaction, so getting our arms around this important facet of our lives is very important.

I created the **Ambition Flowchart** to force myself to stop and consider whether my thoughts, words, and actions are aligned to my Why, which I freely interchange with the words "ambition,"

AMBITION FLOWCHART

"The two most important days of your life are the day you were born and the day you figure out why."

— MARK TWAIN

WHAT IS YOUR AMBITION?
(PURPOSE, CALLING?)

_____
_____

EVERY DAY, WHAT YOU THINK, SAY, AND DO...
DOES IT ALIGN WITH YOUR AMBITION?

NO...
- STOP & REFLECT
- ASSESS WHY
- WHAT NEEDS TO CHANGE?

YES!
- GOOD JOB!
- STAY THE COURSE

Loop 1: Record

"purpose," "calling," and "fire in the belly." Once I really started recording and thinking about these words, I would find them all over — from Bruce Springsteen's book, *Born to Run* where he calls it "your Sword," to Robin Williams in the *Dead Poets Society* where he refers to it as "your Verse."

I typically write two Ambition Flowcharts into each journal to see how my thinking changes over time. When the page comes up in my note-taking sequence, I take

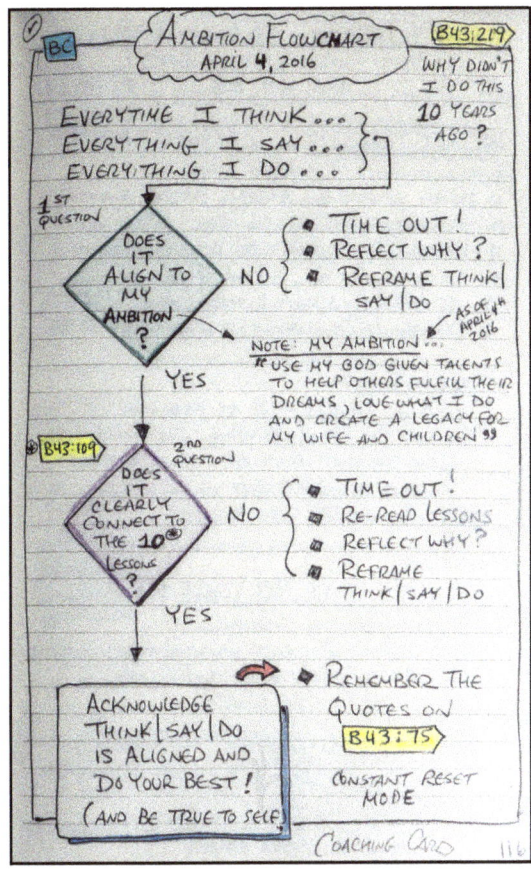

Earlier iteration example of the Ambition Flowchart

time to reflect on where I am, who I want to be, and how to best get there — becoming more comfortable that it can be an attainable moving target.

When I look back over a few journals, I can see that my ambition changes as my thinking and experiences continue to expand. I'm reminded of a relevant quote from Heraclitus:

> "No man stands in the same river twice and just like the river, we are constantly changing and evolving our perceptions every day."

It's also worth noting that conversations on the Ambition Flowchart are the number one discussion topic requested by my mentees as they are pursuing the deeper meanings of their own ambitions.

ALIGNMENT MODEL

The most important decision you make every day is where you spend your time. What do you need to STOP and START doing in order to make your ambition come true?

THINGS I NEED TO STOP:

_____
_____
_____
_____
_____
_____
_____

THINGS I NEED TO START:

_____
_____
_____
_____
_____
_____
_____

Loop 1: Record

In your journal, you'll want to tab a page at the halfway point to remind yourself to create a new Ambition Flowchart. You need not confine yourself to only two Ambition Flowcharts, but it's very important that you routinely perform this reassessment at least twice per journal.

II. ALIGNMENT MODEL – STOP & START

The Start & Stop was recently added to the journals and follows behind the Ambition Flowchart as a reminder to set aside time to really focus my thinking. I needed a way to assess what actions needed to change if my alignment to my ambition veered off target.

In order to see how I was doing, I recorded every decision I made over a two-week period to see how consistent (or inconsistent) I was in staying aligned to my ambition. Tracking your decisions is a very humbling experience, especially when your decision turns out to be completely wrong. Overall, I was on target most of the time but learned how easy it is to lose focus, especially when under pressure from unexpected events.

> **"People need to be reminded more than they need to be instructed."**
> **- Samuel Johnson**

One of the benefits of journaling is that when you determine what you need to start and stop doing, it is typically something you already know, and you just need a reminder as a kick in the pants to get thinking in the more powerful direction.

III. LEADERSHIP RATIOS

By watching and listening to some truly exceptional leaders I learned that leadership is always situational, and the best leaders always adjust their approaches and styles for the best possible outcomes. There are no cookie cutter approaches as every situation is unique.

Effective leaders are constantly adjusting the most important ratios where the numerator and denominator are deliberately set

for the specific situation. For example, on the leadership ratio for Listen/Talk, some leaders feel like they have to tell everyone what to do and they don't listen very well. Their ratio is 80% Talk and 20% Listen, and this usually results in suboptimal outcomes because employees will stop contributing ideas if their leaders do not listen.

I have found that the best Listen/Talk ratio is 80% listening and 20% talking, and the talking is typically in the form of asking insightful questions and gathering intelligence. A slight adjustment between the numerator and denominator is all that's needed go from "good" to "great."

Sometimes a simple ratio can be constructed from a multitude of other "sub-level ratios," which is why it's so hard to master. For example, the Confidence/Arrogance ratio can have the following components involved — if one of them is performed sub optimally, the whole equation is off.

Keep in mind that the ratios are metaphors to help people think about their approaches and not true mathematical expressions.

I've collected over a few hundred ratios in the past decade and detect new ones all the time.

Since I started observing, recording and collecting ratios, I am always creating new ways to understand the leadership impact of multi-component ratios.

For example, one of my mentees asked me my thoughts on what "World Class Communication" looks and feels like. I thought about it for a few days and then built the following ratio model from journal notes on communication best practices.

IV. HEALTH & HAPPINESS CHECK-UP

In the middle of your journal, add a marker that will be your prompt to stop and take stock of your health and personal happiness via the Health and Happiness Check-up (see my template on the next page).

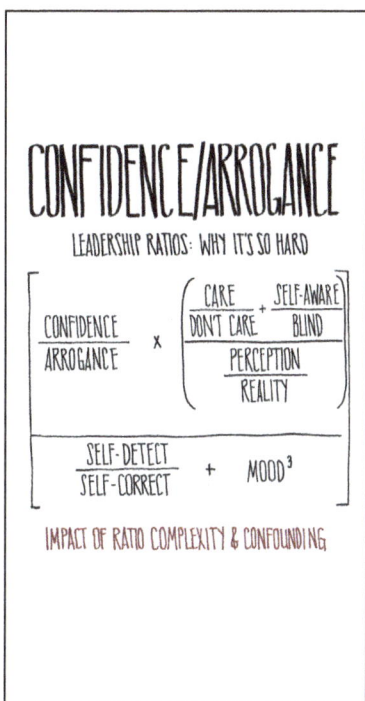

While these are simple yes/no observations, they are incredibly useful for self-examination and improvement. They are also the things we would otherwise neglect unless reminded on a regular basis.

The Health and Happiness Checkup was another recent addition to the journals for me, to ensure that I take time to put aside for a moment the intense focus on leadership learning and do a reflective assessment of my health and personal happiness. A strong body and strong mind are two of the most important assets in leadership. I'm constantly reminded that good health is an important component of good wealth.

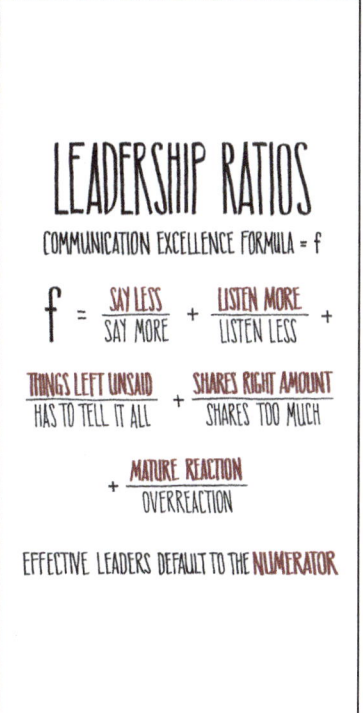

Four Loop Learning: The Art of Journaling and Reflective Leadership

Though these seem on the surface to be inward-facing elements, your health and personal happiness have an enormous impact on yourself and others.

HEALTH & HAPPINESS

DATE OF YOUR ASSESSMENT: _____

	YES	NO		YES	NO
Blood pressure in acceptable range?	☐	☐	Marriage/Partnership strong?	☐	☐
Body mass index (BMI) in range?	☐	☐	Mood under control?	☐	☐
Cholesterol in acceptable range?	☐	☐	Good friendships enduring?	☐	☐
Glucose (sugar level) in range?	☐	☐	Deep connection with children?	☐	☐
Rigorous exercise regime in practice?	☐	☐	Deep connection with family? (parents, siblings)	☐	☐
PSA (men)/Breast exam (women)?	☐	☐	Deep spiritual connection?	☐	☐
Physical in last 12 months?	☐	☐			

LOOP 2: REFLECT

As we learned in the discussion about commonplace books and the importance of memory and learning in general, the real strength of consistent journaling comes as a result of regular review of the material that we are committing to the page. "Repeat to remember" is the mantra.

Stop and Reflect is our way to "remember to repeat," another vital component of information retention.

> "To read without reflecting is like eating without digesting."
> - Edmund Burkes

The way it works is simple: After every 50 pages of your journal, take time to go back over those pages and extract the material you feel is most relevant and important to you going forward. Record them on your Stop & Reflect page.

The Stop & Reflect page also contains a dual directional thinking approach that I refer to as Convergent and Divergent thinking.

CONVERGENT THINKING

In Convergent reflection, I look at my journal notes to see where things tend to meet or converge at a specific point. This is the foundation of how I designed and use the journal.

I reflect and rerecord the key learnings at every one of the Stop & Reflects during dedicated **Reflection Points**. There are four Stop

> "I INSIST ON A LOT OF TIME SPENT, EVERY DAY, TO JUST SIT BACK AND THINK... SO I DO MORE READING AND THINKING."
>
> — WARREN BUFFETT

STOP & REFLECT

- Summarize the most significant learnings from the past 50 pages
- List the page number so you can locate it quickly in a future search
- Cross reference each Stop & Reflect learning to the Head (how you think), Hand (how you do it), and Heart (how you feel) – your H-Link

Example:

KEY LEARNING	REFERENCE	H-LINK
DO YOU HAVE IT? H – HUMILITY A – AUTHENTICITY V – VULNERABILITY E – EMPATHY	B1:244 BOOK: 1 PAGE: 244	HEART HOW YOU INSPIRE OTHERS

Loop 2: Reflect

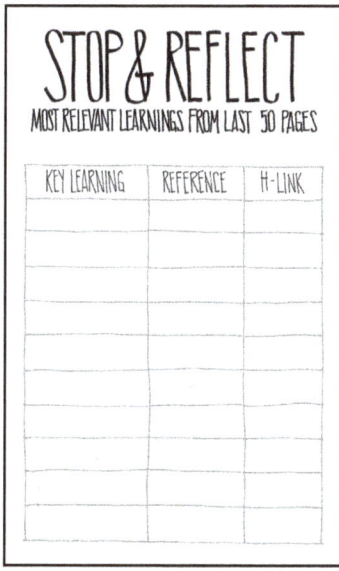

& Reflects in each journal, and I typically capture ~10 learnings per every 50 pages resulting in a total compilation of ~40 learnings per journal.

Then I take the most relevant learning from each of the sets of 50 to get to the top four in the journal. The final step is to narrow down those top four to the number one most important and relevant learning in the entire journal, which I call "Best in Journal."

The benefit of this approach is that it allows me to use the content from multiple entries in a single journal and build out one compelling point of view to then propel into action.

REFLECTION POINT
Deliberate and dedicated time to review journal content with the intent to use the recorded material to solve a problem, create a new coaching model, or just make sense of some leadership puzzle I am trying to figure out.

For example, multiple journals converge when I need to answer "the one thing" — for example, "What one thing can a leader do to really make a big impact?"

Convergent reflection also helped me create what I call "softer side VUCA."

Around 1987, the U.S. Army War College introduced a concept called VUCA to describe the more Volatile, Uncertain, Complex and Ambiguous multilateral world perceived as resulting from the end of the Cold War. The acronym became a management staple soon afterward, and found

> "For purposes of action, nothing is more useful than narrowness of thought combined with energy of will."
> - Henri Frederic Ameil

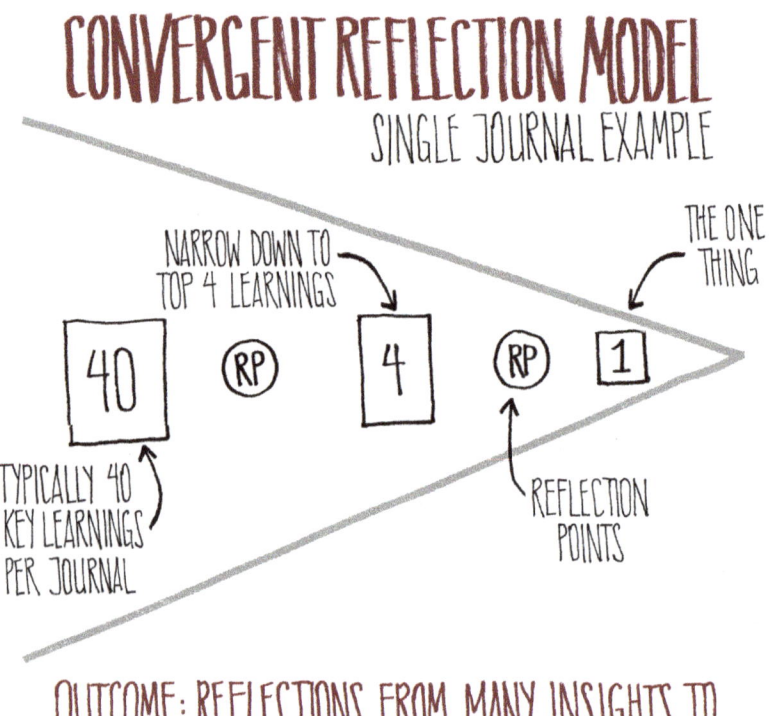

its way into my journaling on multiple occasions as I came across the concept in multiple magazines like *Business Week*, *Harvard Business Review*, *Fortune*, and *Fast Company*.

MULTIPLE VUCA WORDS

HARDWARE IQ	SOFTWARE EQ	AWAKENING
PROFESSIONAL	PERSONAL	ZULU
V - VOLATILE	V - VULNERABLE	V
U - UNCERTAIN	U - UNSELFISH	U
C - COMPLEX	C - CARING	K
A - AMBIGUOUS	A - AUTHENTIC	A
TABLE STAKE SMARTS FOR EXECS	SOFT SKILLS FOR EXPONENTIAL OUTCOMES	SOUTH AFRICAN EXPRESSION: TO "WAKE-UP"

BALANCE ACROSS THE THREE

I felt something was missing. Eventually, I created the a "softer side" VUCA acronym model consisting of Vulnerability, Unselfishness, Care, and Authenticity as the key components of great leadership. These four characteristics kept surfacing multiple times in multiple interpretations throughout my journal notes, and my time taken to Stop and Reflect brought them easily to the surface where I could use them.

I also rediscovered the Zulu word "Vuka" in one of my past journal entries. It means "wake up"— that was too perfect not to include!

Convergent Thinking teamed with regular Reflection Points allowed me to create a new and, I feel, much more leadership-appropriate VUCA acronym. In my experiences, the best leaders I know have a nice balance of both the "hard side" U.S. Army VUCA and my "soft side" VUCA, and this is an area I'm still working on and always curious to learn more about.

DIVERGENT THINKING

In Divergent Reflection, I look at my journal notes to see where my thoughts, research, or observations separate or diverge from one path of thinking and move into a different direction. The benefit here is that throughout the Reflection Points I can propose a specific hypothesis for a leadership challenge I'm trying to solve and then build out lists, trends, or longitudinal points of view to help me test my idea. I also value and record the insights I get from my mentees when I share these points of view with them — getting a reality check on my Divergent Reflection.

> "The larger the island of knowledge, the longer the shoreline of wonder."
> - Ralph Sockman

I typically build out lists that explore executive accelerators and derailers, top 10 reading lists, and key discussion points on a particular subject.

For example: upon reviewing a few dozen journals, here are the top 10 executive accelerators and derailers compiled from multiple studies, presentations, and business magazines in my notes:

Loop 2: Reflect

CHARACTERISTICS THAT ACCELERATE LEADERSHIP IMPACT	CHARACTERISTICS THAT CAN DERAIL LEADERSHIP IMPACT
1. Balance of Hard & Soft VUCA's	1. Makes big decisions without staff dialogue
2. Leads with the right leadership ratios	2. Does not value "devil's advocate" points of view
3. Develops the next generation of leaders	3. Does not invest in their people
4. Inspires and connects versus leading with a command and control framework	4. Not aware of the moods they portray (and bad at setting the right mood)
5. Values the learnings from failure as strategic assets	5. Fails to understand the difficulties in driving change
6. Curious and continuous learner	6. Large degree of arrogance
7. Builds and maintains trust	7. Self-orientation versus a servant leadership orientation
8. Creates an environment of innovation of change	8. Failure to gain fellowship
9. Values dissenting opinions from all levels	9. Relies on overused strengths
10. Inspirational	10. Lack of authenticity and connection to a "deeper why"

REFLECTION THROUGH DIVERGENT THINKING

DIVERGE: SEPARATING FROM ONE ROUTE & GOING IN A DIFFERENT DIRECTION

DIVERGENT REFLECTION MODEL
MULTIPLE JOURNAL EXAMPLE

- CONTENT FROM MULTIPLE JOURNALS
- H — HYPOTHESIS TO THINK ABOUT
- RP — REFLECTION POINTS

1. _____
2. _____
3. _____
4. _____
5. _____
6. _____
7. _____
8. _____
9. _____
10. _____

OUTCOME: REFLECTION OF MANY INSIGHTS TO BUILD LISTS, TRENDS OR LONGITUDINAL POINTS OF VIEW

Loop 2: Reflect

FOUR EXAMPLES OF LOOP TWO JOURNALING ACTIVITIES

I. THE 10 "H'S" OF HIGH IMPACT LEADERSHIP

Multiple years of journaling have taught me that just about everything I record can be applied to one of 10 "H's." These "H's" will reveal themselves throughout your journal and you will soon find it second nature to recognize and record them as soon as they occur.

> "If you want people to have more insights, you need to reduce the overall 'noise' in people's heads and create a space for people to reflect."
> - David Rock

Their secondary benefit is similar to that of the Legend Categories, which you will learn about in the Setting Up Your Journal chapter. Regular tagging of your entries with one of the "H's" will make you mindful of exploring each of these facets of your life's journey during each journaling session.

1. **HAND** – How you get things done.
2. **HAPPINESS** – Your overall mood and disposition.
3. **HEAD** – How you think about things.
4. **HEALTH** – Caring of your mental and physical well-being.
5. **HEART** – What inspires you and how you inspire others.
6. **HELPING** – Coaching others and sharing knowledge to help them become better leaders.
7. **HIGH PERFORMANCE TEAMS** – Building great teams and then sustaining their momentum.
8. **HOPE** – Having only positive expectations.
9. **HORIZONTAL** – Working effectively across organizational departments and breaking through silos.
10. **HUMILITY** – Thinking about yourself less and keeping your ego in check.

In the last column on your Stop & Reflect page, there is a column named the "H-Link" which is used to align your key learning to one of the "H's." By doing this, you will begin to see a pattern of the facets of your life that populate the notes you find most useful and significant — a handy way to keep score.

LEADERSHIP MAXIMS

HEAD: HOW YOU THINK

- Leaders need to be ongoing learners, always curious and constantly learning new things.
- Leaders have to become experts in the marketplaces they serve with effective standard practices of learning, unlearning and relearning with effective knowledge retention practices- whether by memory or quick retrieval systems.
- Leaders have to be resilient and learn to adapt.
- Leaders are deliberately reflective and spend dedicated time to think deeply via timeouts, journaling or via authentic discussions with peers or mentors.
- Leaders create the "What" and the "When" and hire competent people to implement the "How."
- Leaders know that communication has to be in a structure where the messages are impossible to misunderstand.

HAND: WHAT YOU DO

- Leaders need to demonstrate a 30/60/90-day impact plan:
  » 1st 30 days- understand what's working and identify the top areas for improvement
  » 60 days – create a plan to address the most significant pain points and vet with the key influencers for buy-in
  » 90 days – have implemented 1-2 key actions to start making a noticeable difference
- Leaders need to get 3 ratios correct: listen more/talk less, ask more/tell less & people first/profits second.
- Leaders are responsible for identifying, developing and coaching the next wave of leaders.
- Leaders have to be a role model for failure and demonstrate how to get up and recover when fallen down. Fail = First Attempt in Learning.
- Leaders have to surround themselves with people who have strengths and skills that they do not have.
- Leaders know the importance and practice Humility, Authenticity, Vulnerability & Empathy as leadership virtues.
- Leaders know that just because someone makes a mistake, does not mean they are one.
- Leaders know that the learning from failure is a strategic asset for any organization.
- Leaders know that the most harmful word in leadership is Complacency.

HEART: HOW YOU INSPIRE OTHERS

- Leaders know that everyone has a story with an ambition and does not forget that when times are challenging.
- Leaders know they are always a role model for the organization and have to be diligent in what they say and do and how they say it!
- Leaders know that inspiring employees is a critical part of their leadership responsibility.
- Leaders know that people and their purposes (ambitions, callings, etc.) are always more important than profits and process improvements.

Loop 2: Reflect

I've often been fascinated by which "H" reveals itself to be dominant during certain periods of weeks, months, and years. If the 10 "H's" seem to be a bit overwhelming, I recommend you start with the basic three of **Head**, **Heart**, and **Hand**.

Also, once you start thinking about topics in terms of "H" classifications, it will become easier to create new and innovative ways to look at things.

After reviewing multiple journal entries on leadership practices and their alignment to head, hand, and heart, here is a page I created on the leadership maxims which I share within my network.

II. 5-4-3-2-1 NETWORKING AND LEARNING FRAMEWORK

The 5-4-3-2-1 is a networking and learning strategy I created and use to become a better leader with a deeper network of professional expertise. After I attend a formal session, workshop, convention or other networking/learning opportunity, I take some reflective time to look at my journal notes from the event and then complete a formal 5-4-3-2-1. This has proven to be an excellent way to ensure that you derive maximum benefit from these types of opportunities.

Here is how it works: Each one of the numbers has a deliberate meaning and a category to me mindful of as I record notes from the event.

5 – WHO ARE THE FIVE MOST VALUABLE PEOPLE TO ADD TO MY PROFESSIONAL NETWORK WHERE WE HAVE COMPLEMENTARY SKILLS TO HELP EACH OTHER OUT?

One of the biggest lessons I've learned is the power of a strong network and how surrounding yourself with a large cadre of professionals can help each other become successful and reap big advantages.

I use the following criteria to assess the professionals I add to my network:

- ✓ Proven expertise in areas I have a deficit
- ✓ People who can connect the dots. I have found in my experience that only ~5% of the people I work with can see the bigger picture
- ✓ Speak the virtues of others and do not complain about their vices without offering solutions
- ✓ Constantly curious and show commitment to lifetime learning
- ✓ Mindful of their moods and the moods they are setting
- ✓ Willingness to share
- ✓ Environmentally conscious
- ✓ Have to courage to ask for help
- ✓ Committed to help others less fortunate in the world
- ✓ They are just an overall good person with whom I enjoy spending time

10 BOOKS
THAT INFLUENCED MY JOURNALING

1. **What Got You Here Won't Get You There**
   by Marshall Goldsmith
   Why? Exposes 21 dysfunctional leadership behaviors to avoid

2. **Good to Great**
   by Jim Collins
   Why? Level 5 Leadership is a great goal

3. **The Speed of Trust**
   by Stephen M.R. Covey
   Why? Great formula on Trust (Strategy x Execution) Trust = Results

4. **The First 90 Days**
   by Michael Watkins
   Why? STAR Model to determine the situation you are in

5. **Great Failures of the Extremely Successful**
   by Steve Young
   Why? Great learning: failure is your friend

6. **Leadership Challenge**
   by Kouzes & Posner
   Why? Incredible insight on what Leadership is and is not

7. **The Five Dysfunctions of a Team**
   by Patrick Lencioni
   Why? Shares the importance of vulnerability

8. **Creative Approaches to Problem Solving**
   by Scott Isaksen
   Why? Great framework for creating innovation and change

9. **Emotional Intelligence 2.0**
   by Travis Bradberry
   Why? Critical importance of the soft skills in leadership

10. **The Decision Book**
    by Mikael Krogerus
    Why? 50 strategic models that always come in handy

Loop 2: Reflect

EVENT:_____ DATE:_____   EVENT:_____ DATE:_____

5-4-3-2-1   # 5-4-3-2-1

5 THE FIVE MOST POWERFUL PROFESSIONALS TO ADD TO YOUR NETWORK:
1._____
2._____
3._____
4._____
5._____

4 THE FOUR MOST IMPORTANT THINGS YOU LEARNED FROM THIS SESSION:
1._____
2._____
3._____
4._____

THE THREE MOST IMPORTANT THINGS YOU LEARNED TO ACCELERATE YOUR AMBITION AND THE AMBITION OF OTHERS: **3**
1._____
2._____
3._____

THE TWO THINGS YOU DID WELL AS A LEADER, AND TWO THINGS YOU CAN DO BETTER: **2**
1._____
2._____ (DID WELL)
1._____
2._____ (DO BETTER)

IF YOU LOOK BACK TEN YEARS FROM NOW, WHAT IS THE ONE THING YOU WILL REMEMBER: **1**
1._____

4 – WHAT ARE THE 4 MOST IMPORTANT THINGS I LEARNED DURING THIS EVENT?

I review my notes and locate the 4 most relevant learnings from the session(s). Many times, the most important learnings are recorded once again in the Stop & Reflect exercises that occur every 50 pages; it's OK if they are rerecorded a few times as it just keeps on reinforcing the most important learnings.

3 – WHAT ARE THE 3 MOST IMPORTANT THINGS YOU LEARNED TO ACCELERATE YOUR AMBITION AND THE AMBITION OF OTHERS?

When I attend meetings, I try to keep a perceptive eye on key learnings that can accelerate my ambition or help others. After I record these thoughts, I quickly vet them against my Ambition Flowchart from the first RECORD Loop to ensure

> "If I could ask only one question in an hour, I would spend 55 minutes on what the question should be."
>
> - Albert Einstein

that my actions are aligned to my ambition. This constant validation really helps me stay focused on things of primary importance, and the Start & Stop questions connected to the Ambition Flowchart are very helpful to maintain the right course.

2 – WHAT ARE 2 THINGS I FELT I DID WELL AS A LEADER AND WHAT ARE THE TWO THINGS I CAN DO BETTER NEXT TIME?

This is a bifurcated question with which I have learned so much about myself throughout the years. I record my perception of what I'm doing well and also record what I could have done better. I look at my notes on my areas for improvement and then try my best to mitigate against them in my next 5-4-3-2-1 opportunity. This habit keeps me very humble and serves as a constant reminder that improvement is a journey that requires a lifetime of dedication.

With that in mind, I took a look at eight journals over the past decade with 28 self-observations.

On the "WHAT DID I DO WELL" analysis (see page 86), I built a quick pareto of my responses. Passion and enthusiasm came up as a capability that I perceived was valued by the participants by virtue of their positive responses. I've learned that enthusiasm is definitely a force multiplier.

> "Every great and commanding movement in the annals of the world is due to the triumph of enthusiasm."
> - Ralph Waldo Emerson

On the "WHAT CAN I DO BETTER" analysis (see page 87), the pareto of my responses indicated that I have to do a much better job aligning my messages and key points to their most significant and specific challenges.

One of the new practices I've started is a review of my WHAT CAN I DO BETTER list before the next engagement commences. Focusing on improvement areas keeps you quite humble.

Loop 2: Reflect

The assessment of what you can do better can also be formalized into an Individual Development Plan where you work to keep an ongoing focus on your commitment to improvement. You improve one thing and then start working on another.

One of the many benefits of journaling is that it gives you the space to reflect and do some deep thinking on how to improve these developmental focus areas. The *Harvard Business Review's* Michael Porter and Nitin Nohria feel that it's vital for CEO's to block off meaningful amounts of uninterrupted time alone, to give themselves space to think, reflect, and prepare.

1 – IF I COULD PROJECT 10 YEARS INTO THE FUTURE AND LOOK BACK AT THIS EVENT, WHAT WOULD BE THE NUMBER ONE MOST IMPORTANT THING TO REMEMBER?

Typically, a 5-4-3-2-1 will be accompanied by a dozen pages of notes. No one can remember and successfully act on so many ideas, so I try to focus on that *one most important learning* from this specific engagement that can positively impact my leadership capability for the rest of my life.

I did some additional analysis on 27 journals over a five-year period that contained 68 unique 5-4-3-2-1's. Here are a few observations to share on this personal analysis:

- The identification of adding five professionals to your network at every event is a great way to expand your professional reach! 68 separate 5-4-3-2-1's means 340 professionals have been added to my network (68 X 5). That is a lot of experts I can connect with to gain advice on just about any leadership issue that needs tackling. One of the most critical points here is that I do not need to know everything about leadership development, I just need to know who to ask when I don't know — a vast network does that for you.

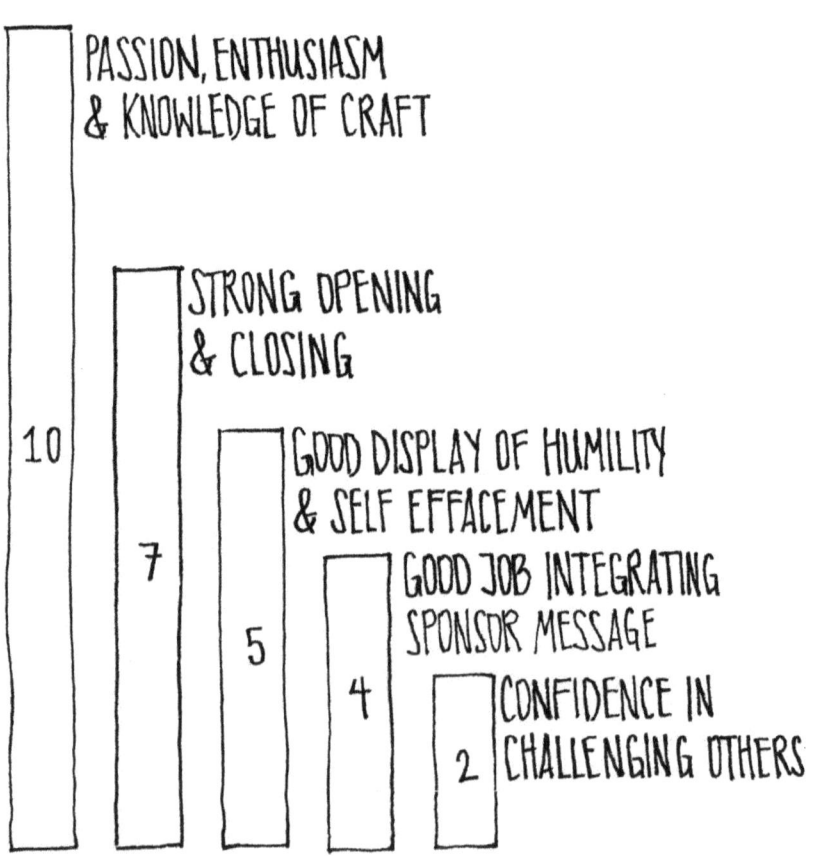

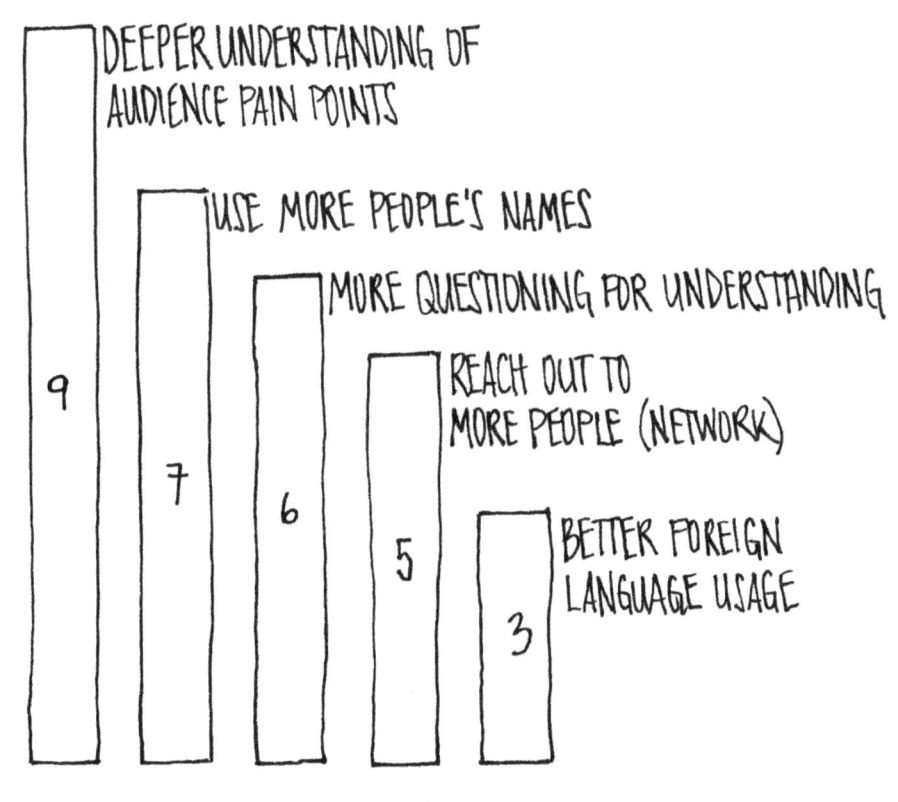

Four Loop Learning: The Art of Journaling and Reflective Leadership

- The recording of what you can do better is a nice way to keep on "upping your game." I'd rather take a serious approach and own my improvement than be constantly told by someone else.

Regarding the #1 most significant learning from the 5-4-3-2-1's, I also keep track of these learnings and categorize them to the 3 H's of Head, Heart, & Hand. I always learn so much about myself as I do this. Here is what my data revealed:

HEAD	HEART	HAND
32%	25%	43%

During these 68 sessions, "HAND" seemed to be my dominant trait. It's interesting, then, to think about whether this was the most optimal approach during these sessions and if I need to adjust my approach going forward.

> "It isn't what people think is important, but the reason they think what they think."
> - Eugene Ionesco

I also like to compare the dominant "H" from the 5-4-3-2-1 to the "H" from the one most significant learning or "Best in Journal" in the entire journal. So far I have different "H's" coming up all over the place!

III. LEVERAGE RULE – AKA FORCE MULTIPLICATION

The 10X (or 10 times) leverage rule is a metaphor for thinking bigger and bolder versus pursuing only a 10% better result. The 10X metaphor is similar to the term "Force Multiplier."

Where can you activate a leadership action that can yield a multi-point benefit?

10 TIMES LEVERAGE RULE

Most people and companies pursue only a 10% improvement. Great leaders and companies pursue a 10 times better mindset in their thinking, idea generation, and actions.

What can you do to achieve results in a way that generates a 10 times improvement or impact?

_____
_____
_____
_____
_____
_____
_____

One example is in the deliberate cascade of information related to approval levels. When big decisions required approval for the next upper level of management, I would write my e-mail requests to my boss with all of the details so all he had to do was forward to his boss for approval. The e-mail typically had a quick summary of the pros and cons, a summary of the research completed, and a very specific request that included an ROI and timeline on the requested activity. Again, it's one well thought-out e-mail that resulted in a quicker decision as you help your boss win faster with their boss — thats the multiplication effect!

> "I don't focus on what I'm up against. I focus on my goals and ignore the rest."
> - Venus Williams

THE POWER OF A BLANK SHEET OF PAPER

Many times, throughout my career, one of my employees would come into my office, share some perspectives on an issue they were dealing with, and then would ask me, "Boss, what should I do?"

I would take out a blank sheet of paper and we would map out the problem, brainstorm solutions, agree on the pros and cons of each solution, and then get it down to one tangible action item for them to go out and implement.

Just before they walked out of my office, I would ask them to consider something for the future: Come to the meeting with the blank sheet of paper already completed with their recommended solution(s).

This really helped my team think things through at a deeper level and solve our challenges with a faster outcome.

IV. INVERTED LOGIC COACHING INSIGHTS

As I come across quotes or phrases that use inversion to make a salient point, I record them into the journals as a category. I find nuances in their meanings to be very helpful in coaching sessions when I want to share a new paradigm of how to think differently about challenges that my mentees are encountering.

Loop 2: Reflect

Similar to adjusting the numerator or denominator of a ratio to dramatically enhance impact, the slight nuance in the interpretation of these quotes can be such a powerful way to help shift a paradigm for higher impact thinking.

For example, the dysfunctional leadership behavior of always having to have the last word in a meeting because you have to show you are the smartest person in the room is a perfect place to use this quote:

"It's not how smart you are, it's how you are smart."

The coaching discussion would begin by calling out the behavior in a private conversation and seeing if they notice the negative body language exhibited from their team (i.e. rolling their eyes). Then the second step would be figuring out some alternative ways to try a different "how" for a better outcome.

I've collected so many of these Inverted Logic insights over the last 10 years that I have a dedicated journal just for these quotes with over 100 captured in Journal 30. Here are eight of my favorites:

COACHING ON:

ARROGANCE
"Humility is not thinking less of yourself; it's thinking about yourself less."
- The Servant

EFFECTIVE PRESENTATIONS
"It's not about getting through the stuff; it's about getting the stuff through."
- Anonymous

CONFIDENCE
"Don't let your doubts control the future, instead control the future of your doubts."
- Anonymous

CARING ABOUT EMPLOYEES
"People don't care how much you know until they know how much you care."
- Theodore Roosevelt

IDEA GENERATION
"The best way forward is the authority of ideas, NOT the ideas of authority."
- Anonymous

PERSPECTIVE
"Do you see a world of wonder or do you wonder what you see?"
- Fisher-Price

PERSEVERANCE
"The best way out is always through."
- Robert Frost

LEADERSHIP
"Management is doing things right, leadership is doing the right things."
- Peter F. Drucker

LOOP 3: ACT

While it may seem self-evident that we take action with the benefit of new information and ideas, I think that if we all look realistically into our daily actions we recognize that it's easy to become complacent.

One way to stimulate action is in the final examination we do at the end of each journal. When you get to the closing page of a now-filled journal, it's time to go back yet again to look over your Stop & Reflects and tabbed pages to determine, before inaugurating a new journal, what was your "Best in Journal?"

It takes three steps to come up with your one "Best in Journal" to put into action.

STEP 1: BEST OF THE 50'S – NARROWING DOWN TO YOUR TOP 4 LEARNINGS WITH ONE FROM EACH SET OF 50

Start with listing your Stop & Reflect entries; if you have a 250-page journal you'll typically have four sets to write out as they occur at every 50-page mark. For each set, write out the one that you believe is the most significant learning for every 50 pages at this point in time, getting you to a list of four key learnings.

Congratulations — you have taken a formidable amount of information and made it accessible and useful!

> "GREATNESS IS NOT A FUNCTION OF CIRCUMSTANCE. GREATNESS, AS IT TURNS OUT, IS LARGELY A MATTER OF CONSCIOUS CHOICE AND DISCIPLINE."
>
> — JIM COLLINS

Four Loop Learning: The Art of Journaling and Reflective Leadership

BEST IN JOURNAL

LOOK AT EACH OF THE STOP & REFLECTS COMPLETED EVERY 50 PAGES AND SELECT THE MOST RELEVANT FROM EACH ONE.

	KEY LEARNING	REFERENCE	H-LINK
50			
100			
150			
200			

Keep in mind that your key learning will be circumstantial during this moment. Things can be more or less relevant and entirely different a few weeks or months from now. That's the beauty of the method — seeing your perspectives and learnings evolve over time.

Now, armed with this powerful trove of data, you will be able to address Loop Three by narrowing down one more time to the most important learning in the entire journal.

However, in addition to finding the one most important learning, you can practice a bunch of smaller new ideas with mini Change Statements. When you decide that you want to try something different, go ahead and create a Change Statement to bring to your new journals – and, of course, to your daily work and life.

There's a species of new and altered habits that many people refer to as "life hacks." Life hacks are informal tips, tricks, shorthands, or efficient methods for doing or managing a day-to-day task or activity. Online you'll find subcultures devoted to these sorts of small-to-large "secret weapons" that are shared among dedicated "life hackers."

> *"If people knew how hard I worked to get my mastery, it would not seem so wonderful at all."*
>
> *- Michelangelo*

For example, if you Google "Best Life Hacks," you may find that the very first entry is: "Before you discard a Post-it® Note, run the adhesive side between your keyboard keys to pick up crumbs and fluff." Handy, but not exactly what we are after.

Loop 3: Act

Your chosen Change Statement should consist of behaviors and habits — big or small — that will make you a:

- **Better, healthier person, friend and family member**
- **More effective leader**
- **More creative thinker**
- **Better influencer to those around you**
- **Quicker producer of quality work**
- **Higher impact decision maker**

The goal is to use the journal to be mindful of these changes and to capture your progress. Practice on smaller things will provide you with experience and confidence to tackle bigger challenges.

STEP 2: BEST IN JOURNAL – THE ONE MOST IMPORTANT LEARNING

The Best in Journal will end up being the one most relevant learning in the entire journal that you will want to put into action.

Take the list of the top four from Step 1 and now narrow it down again to the *single most significant learning*…which is very hard to do because you have given yourself so much relevant material to choose from!

> **BEST IN JOURNAL**
>
> The most relevant and impactful learning in this journal is…

Getting it down to one key lesson is not easy, and it's been getting tougher for me as I keep on journaling; there are just too many terrific learnings to choose from!

At this point, I say: "Congratulations — what a great problem to have!" I like to refer to this as having a "positive breakdown" because you have so many great learnings you can choose from. One of my goals with my mentees is to help them have as many positive breakdowns as possible. For example, what a nice breakdown it would be to have five different companies aggressively pursuing you to join their organization at the same time.

STEP 3: WHAT'S THE ONE THING?

OK, here is what this journal is all about: taking action to improve your impact as a leader.

What will be the one (and only one) thing that you can focus on to take your leadership to a higher level of performance?

> **WHAT'S THE ONE THING?**
>
> *"THE PROBLEM WITH EXECUTION IS NOT THE ABSENCE OF KNOWING WHAT TO DO, BUT THE ABSENCE OF DOING IT."*
> — PETER DRUCKER
>
> TAKE SOME DEEP REFLECTION TIME TO LOOK AT YOUR NOTES AND FIND THE ONE THING THAT REALLY RESONATED WITH YOU, THAT IF IMPLEMENTED TOMORROW WOULD ENHANCE YOUR LEADERSHIP CAPABILITY IN A NOTICEABLE WAY:
>
> I WILL DO: _____
>
> AS MEASURED BY: _____
>
> BY DATE: _____
>
> **THEN JUST DO IT AND SHARE WITH OTHERS!**

As Thomas Edison stated: *"The first requisite for success is to develop the ability to focus and apply your mental and physical energies to the problem at hand without growing weary."*

The most important next step is to *do something…and do it now!* Then, use the next Journal to assess how you are doing. If you are successful, take some time and celebrate your accomplishment. If you are not, well, just Stop & Reflect, and try again.

When you have a productive mindset and things go awry, the learnings from failure are your friend, not the end!

Loop 3: Act

THREE EXAMPLES OF LOOP THREE JOURNALING ACTIVITIES

I. BOB'S RESEARCH ON THE H-LINKS FROM THE ONE THINGS OF MULTIPLE JOURNALS

I was really curious to see what I would learn about myself if I looked back over the last 20 or so journals to see specifically what I recorded as the most significant Journal learning, especially as cross referenced to the three H's of Hand, Head, & Heart.

The analysis of multiple journals revealed that my most significant learnings fell into the distribution at right.

Looks like my leadership is heavily aligned to heartfelt practices. I was not surprised that my heart percentage was highest because my deep care for my team and my mentees is typically what they said they value in me.

The one concern in being a leader with a dominant "H"- Heart is that you have to ensure that you have a good balance of the other H's to become a high performance team. I had to be careful that my heavy emphasis on Heart did not overtake the importance of other "H" capabilities — things like the importance of data in decision making in the Head classification, and the ability to get things done in the Hand classification.

II. LEGENDARY – WHAT DO YOU WANT YOUR T-SHIRT TO SAY

As you complete each journal, you will find that you have gained an incredible amount of new and deeper perspective around the way you think, feel, and act.

WHAT DO YOU WANT YOUR LEGEND TO BE?

It's your retirement day and the key people in your career are about to present you with a t-shirt with a sentence that sums up the impact you have made throughout your career.

WHAT WOULD YOU LIKE YOUR T-SHIRT TO SAY?

Loop 3: Act

One of the coaching exercises that my mentees find valuable is to create a Retirement Legacy statement. This is done by defining, in 25 words or less, what they would like people to remember them for as they wave goodbye and transition into retirement.

If the word "retirement" is a bit to alien to persons in the early stages of their career, I use these other phrases as well across the generational types:

Millennial: "What's your hashtag?"

Gen X: "What's your billboard going to say?"

Boomers: "What will they say is your t-shirt?"

Post Retirement: "What will you be known for when you are 68?"

Epitaph: "What would you like on your tombstone?

I've created a continuum of legacy (aka COL) to show how these questions might look over time.

The objective is to assess whether their current behaviors align to their stated future legacy. Your future legacy is the summation of all the leadership practices you do each and every day.

> **"The great aim of education is not knowledge, but action."**
> **- Herbert Spencer**

I once worked with a team who confidently shared that their bosses t-shirt would be the following:

SAYS YES, THINKS NO, & DOES NOTHING

Knowing that one of the fundamental credos in facilitating is never leaving a team in worse shape than where you started, I transitioned this group to coming up with the specific behaviors that could turn the situation around into the following future state t-shirt:

BEST BOSS EVER WHO LISTENED

What a great time to self-correct your behaviors today for the tomorrow you would like to see on your t-shirt. Even better is asking for your team's inputs on how to do it, which displays great vulnerability.

On a personal note: I'm mindful and working my absolute hardest to ensure that my future t-shirt would say something like this:

> "He Listened, He Inspired, He Cared
> and WE DELIVERED!

If this is the impression I leave, then I would assess that I've had one heck of a successful career and great impact as a leader.

III. DO YOU HAVE IT?

At the end of keynote presentations where I share many different points of view on leadership from the journals, I typically get asked the following question:

"Bob, you just shared a ton of perspective with us. At its simplest, what is the one model in your opinion that creates the most effective leaders?"

Knowing that IQ is a prerequisite for any person in an executive role along with deep industry knowledge, the model that I created is based upon a very simple question: Do you have it?

DO YOU **HAVE** IT?

Where…

JOURNAL REFLECTION

DO YOU HAVE IT?

- **H** – HUMILITY
- **A** – AUTHENTICITY
- **V** – VULNERABILITY
- **E** – EMPATHY

AND IF NOT, WHEN?

- **W** – WHAT WILL YOU DO?
- **H** – HOW WILL YOU DO IT?
- **E** – ENERGY PUT INTO IT?
- **N** – NEVER REST ON YOUR LAURELS

> **H** = Humility – "It's not thinking less of yourself, it's less thinking of yourself"
>
> **A** = Authenticity – "Bringing your whole self to work"
>
> **V** = Vulnerability – "Showing that you are not perfect and that you are OK with that"
>
> **E** = Empathy – "People don't care how much you know until they know how much you care"

And, to then help those who feel they don't HAVE it yet, I ask them **WHEN**?

Where…

> **W** = What will you do and what is your plan?
>
> **H** = How will you do it and who in your network can help?
>
> **E** = What energy will you put into it and what will be your say/do ratio on action?
>
> **N** = Never rest on your laurels as leadership development is a lifelong project.

In my observation, there are essential capabilities that are a prerequisite to be successful in C-Suite roles, and sometimes these are referred to as the "hard skills," which I refer to as the ticket-entry skills or table stakes which are critical to perform effectively in senior leadership roles.

Once you have demonstrated these hard skills, you can then assess whether you HAVE it or not on the soft skills.

KEY TICKET-ENTRY EXECUTIVE CAPABILITIES
- High IQ
- Strong network and networking skills
- Industry expertise
- Strategic thinker

Loop 3: Act

- Hard work ethic
- Good judgment skills
- Asks insightful questions
- Courage to disrupt
- Context for digital and big data
- Smart risk taker

If you have the hard skills, then you can see if you HAVE the soft skills as both are needed for successful leadership. If you do, that's great and keep on refining them. If not, then determine WHEN you will and what you will do to obtain them.

There is another question that I get asked: "What if I had it and then I lose it?"

I used a similar approach to review the contents from myriad journals to come up with this model for people to reflect upon.

L = Lost touch of reality or Leading with complacency
O = Overused strength or Only value "yes" people
S = Stopped listening or Selfishness took over your Servant leadership style
E = Ego is out of control or your Executive presence is exhibiting unproductive behaviors

Journaling can help you pinpoint some of the reasons you lost what you had by really reflecting deeply on why these are occurring. It's slowing down to better understand, and then making changes to enhance your leadership performance.

LOOP 4: SHARE

The final loop in my journaling sequence is one that is particularly important to me because I've made a career of sharing and teaching leadership skills. My primary goal in gathering information, in fact, is to find valuable material and ways to pass along that information to others to help them fulfill their leadership ambitions.

However, you do not have to be an educator, business coach, or session leader to reap the benefits of the fourth loop. In fact, research has shown that one of the best ways to learn and perfect a skill is to challenge yourself to teach that skill to someone else.

> "Knowing is not enough; we must apply. Willing is not enough; we must do."
> - Johann Wolfgang von Goethe

As my favorite author Mark Twain said, "It is noble to teach oneself, but still nobler to teach others." We have already noted that retention and memory is increased by employing "loops" that re-engage the material. In her book *Corporate Universities*, researcher Jeanne Meister created a pyramid detailing the benefits of action-based learning — loops by another name.

At the bottom of the list of retention rates (5%) is *Lecture*; things just do not stick very well when they are simply "spewed" in your direction. The list progresses through better and better retention results: *Reading* (10%); *Audio-Visual* (20%); *Demonstration* (30%); and *Discussion Group* (50%).

> **FOR IT IS IN GIVING THAT WE RECEIVE.**
>
> — FRANCIS OF ASSISI

The run-away winners, however, are *Practice by Doing* at a whopping 75%, exceeded only by *Teach Others* at 80%.

A friend of mine told me about a great example in his own life of using teaching or sharing to aid retention of information. He recently got interested in photography again after decades away from it and treated himself to a new and complicated camera. Its capabilities are mind-boggling, and the myriad menus and controls baffled my friend to the extent he bought some books about the device and watched dozens of YouTube videos to unlock the camera's secrets and become more comfortable with it. He also journaled elemental concepts like exposure, shutter speed, ISO, digital processing, etc. as he encountered them. He reviewed his notes regularly.

Writing notes on the material he learned was a great help. He also noticed that actually *doing* something he read about or saw demonstrated — getting "hands-on" and going into the back yard to shoot a night time-lapse after reading about the procedure, for instance — greatly increased his ability to grasp and remember the steps required to accomplish the task.

The real breakthrough did not occur until his daughter began a photography class in high school and expressed interest in his new camera. Soon, he regularly took time to teach his daughter the things he'd read in a book or seen via online video. In addition to making photography that much more fun because he was sharing it with his daughter, he found that teaching made the information "stickier"— that is, much easier to remember and retain.

SIX EXAMPLES OF LOOP FOUR JOURNALING ACTIVITIES AS EXAMPLES OF APPLIED TEACHING

I. WHERE MENTEES ASK FOR HELP

Over the past five years, I've collected the top five leadership pain points from 55 mentees I've been working with to help enhance their leadership capabilities and accelerate the path to their career ambitions.

The mentees were a nice cross section of Gen X'ers and Millennials, and their top five concerns range from career navigation to dealing with a challenging Manager. These are typically the key developmental focus areas in the conversations we have, with a prime opportunity to co-create solutions that help them become more aware, learn some new behaviors, and continue their journey to better leadership skills.

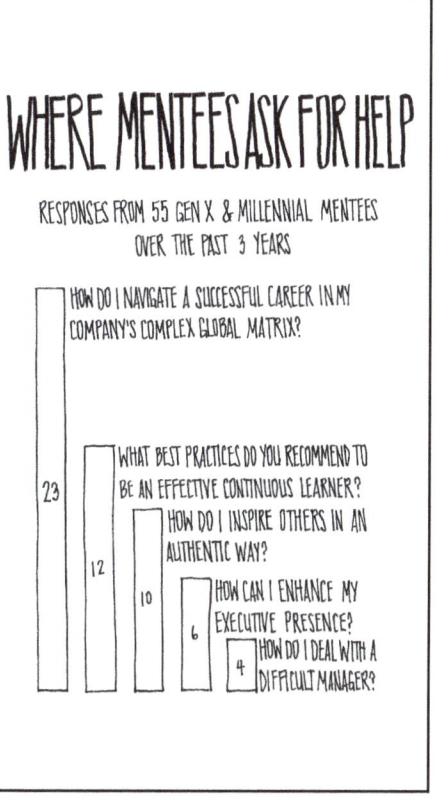

Regarding the third pareto bar, "HOW DO I INSPIRE OTHERS IN AN AUTHENTIC WAY?", I created a formula on Inspiration (see page 108) derived from multiple journal entries, using it to share what I consider the important elements in being more Inspirational.

II. CO-CREATION OF SOLUTIONS

One of the most common uses of my journal contents are when my mentees and I co-create possible solutions to specific leadership challenges they are experiencing.

> "Let us remember one book, one pen, one child, and one teacher can change the world."
> - Malala Yousafzai

We first agree on a single topic that requires a higher impact approach than what they are currently doing. Here's an example involving teaching enhancement of listening skills — a common challenge. It has five very simple steps:

Four Loop Learning: The Art of Journaling and Reflective Leadership

STEP 1: We agree and write down what great listening looks and feels like. For example: GREAT LISTENING SKILLS

- **Deeply connected eye contact**
- **Listening to what is being said – and what is NOT being said**
- **Fully cognizant of their body language**
- **Can parrot back key points**
- **Does not cut people off mid-sentence - lets them finish**
- **Checks for understanding**

STEP 2: We now discuss the extreme opposite: What does the absolute worst listening skills look and feel like? We agree and write that down as well.

For example: REALLY BAD LISTENING SKILLS

- **Thinking about your response as you are being spoken to**
- **Multi-tasking during the conversation (i.e.: reading e-mail, surfing mobile device, looking around)**
- **Body language showing low engagement**
- **Could not repeat back main point of the conversation**
- **Only asks closed ended questions to avoid long answers**

ELEMENTS OF INSPIRATION

$$INSPIRATION = f(P^4 + C + V + H)^B$$

WHERE
P^4 = PEOPLE & PASSION > PROFITS & PROCESS
C = CARE ABOUT YOUR PEOPLE – LOVE 'EM UP!
V = VALUE GOOD & BAD NEWS WITH THE SAME INTENSITY
H = HAVE THEIR BACKS – ESPECIALLY WITH FAILURE
B = BE CONSISTENT

STEP 3: Then, if "Great" is a 5 and "Really Bad" is a 1, I ask my mentee where they think they are on that continuum at this point in time. It's consistent that most conversations result in a mentee's self-proclaimed score of 3, which is a humble response, and a goal of getting to 4.5, knowing a perfect 5 may be unattainable.

Loop 4: Share

STEP 4: I then ask my mentee to brainstorm a bunch of specific behaviors they need to exhibit to move from a 3 to a 4.5. We agree on one or two very specific actions and they build out an action plan.

I have them complete the following action line:

By (specific date) _____,

I will do _____

As measured by _____

... which is very similar to WHAT'S THE ONE THING as explained on page 96.

STEP 5: I reconnect with them after a month or so and see how they are doing and ask what else I can do to help them become successful.

It's really that simple, yet the practice of moving from a 3 to a 5 is very difficult. As stated earlier, when you are successful in your pursuit for better listening skills — celebrate! When you falter a bit or just mess it up — no problem. Just Stop & Reflect and try it again!

Here are the top 10 requests from my mentees over the past decade on helping them co-create solutions to these challenges:

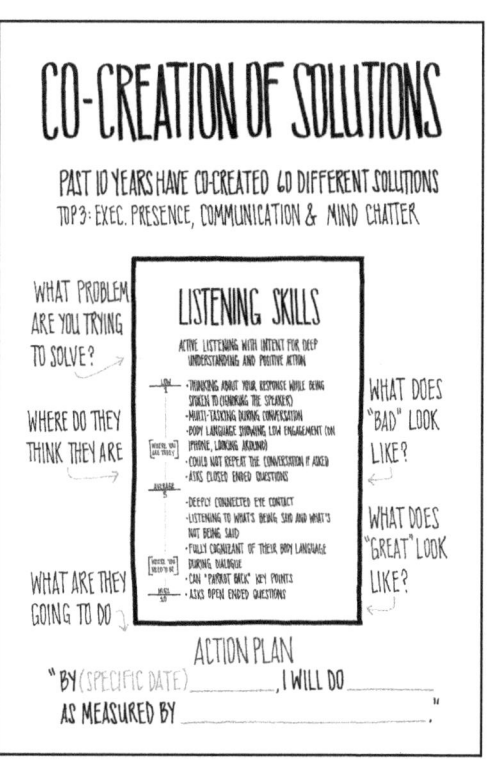

Four Loop Learning: The Art of Journaling and Reflective Leadership

1. **LISTENING SKILLS** – what great listening skills look like
2. **EXECUTIVE PRESENCE** – having a confident and centered body
3. **COMMUNICATION EXCELLENCE** – being brief, being bright, and then being gone
4. **MOOD MANAGEMENT** - how to set the right mood for the right intended outcome
5. **MENTAL CHATTER** – addressing negative mind chatter
6. **HUMILITY** – not crossing the haughty or hubris line
7. **AUTHENTICITY** – having the courage to be your true self
8. **EMPATHY** – really caring for others and understanding their situations
9. **VULNERABILITY** – being comfortable with not knowing it all
10. **SELF-AWARENESS** – knowing how you come across and how to adjust if needed

III. RESILIENCY DEFINITION

> "The best teacher is one who suggests rather than dogmatizes, and inspires his listener with the wish to teach himself."
>
> - Edward Bulwer-Lytton

During my medical journey highlighted in the first chapter, one of my mentees asked me my thoughts on what *resiliency* means. I perused a dozen journals looking for notes on resiliency, adaptability, strength, character, and adversity and then came up with the following definition as an amalgamation of many different thoughts and observations:

Resiliency is a leadership mindset.

It's an inner strength that allows you to learn from tough times and get back up when you have fallen.

It's having the confidence that you can endure today's challenges knowing there will be better days tomorrow.

Resilient leaders learn from adversity and deeply grow in confidence and character when they overcome it.

The art of journaling helped me quickly locate material in multiple journals which made this definition possible.

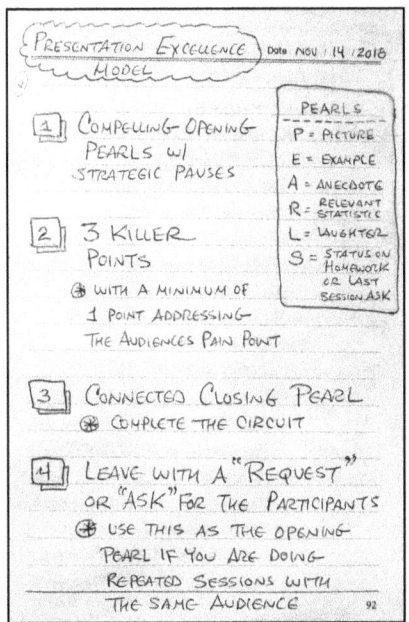

IV. MODEL FOR DESIGNING COMPELLING KEYNOTES

There have been numerous times when one of my mentees calls in a bit of a panic and informs me they have been selected to give a big presentation on some important topic to senior management.

They ask if I have any coaching on how to prepare and structure a compelling presentation.

Here is a journal page showing a model that was created to help design and deliver an effective presentation which starts with a compelling opening, weaves an integrated story that addresses the pain points of the audience, and then connects back into a compelling closing.

V. MY SIMPLE PHILOSOPHY

My Simple Philosophy on page 112 was created when one of my mentors asked me if my perspective on life has altered in any way as a result of my medical journey.

As I reflected upon my experience in beating head and neck cancer and looked over my journals from the period, I can confirm without a doubt that my philosophy has indeed changed.

This page was created to show how much of my perspective has been transformed via the lenses of Head, Heart, and Hand.

A SIMPLE PHILOSOPHY TO AIM FOR

A successful life is to know:

That I'm inspiring others with my actions and providing them with hope and optimism about their futures and the impact they have on others. (Hand)

That my family always knows that everything I do for them is based upon my never-ending love, unconditional support and lifetime commitment to them. (Heart)

That I matter and am relevant in what I do. (Hand)

That my words are warm and caring with the appropriate tones and responses tightly aligned to the situation encountered. (Head)

That my friends have a few good stories to share to keep my integrity and authenticity alive. (Heart)

That the summation of my successes and failures in life are defining who I am and who I'm working on becoming to realize my God given potential. (Hand)

That I'm working on leaving a positive legacy for my children and my children's children. (Hand)

That I'm so grateful for every day for all of the gifts I have been given. (Heart)

That I continue to have a servant leadership headset in how I think and what I do and never to forget that responsibility. (Hand)

And that I understand my entire life was in God's hands from the start and that I'm doing my best knowing that God will do the rest. (Heart)

Loop 4: Share

VI. MODEL OF THE FIVE I'S OF LEADERSHIP

This model provides a detailed example of the additive nature of journaling and how easy it can be to expand upon an original idea or concept.

> "The evidence, scientific as well as anecdotal, seems overwhelmingly in favor of deliberate practice as a source of great performance."
> - Geoffrey Colvin

5-I MODEL   Date DEC / 29 / 2018

EFFECTIVE LEADERSHIP = I^5

INSPIRATION
$I = f(P^3 + C + V + H)^c$

- P^3 - PEOPLE'S PASSION; PURPOSE
- C - CARE ABOUT THEM
- V - VALUE GOOD AND BAD NEWS
- H - HAVE THEIR BACKS
- c - CONSISTENT IN YOUR APPROACH

INTEGRITY
$I = f(R + N + P^3 + C^N + W)$

- R - RIGHT THING
- N - NOBODY IS WATCHING
- P^3 - PEOPLE, PEOPLE, PEOPLE
- C^N - CONFIDENTIALITY NOBODY, NOTHING, NEVER
- W - WALL STREET JOURNAL TEST

INTELLIGENCE
$I = V^H + V^S + EI + S$

- V^H - VUCA - HARD
- V^S - VUCA - SOFT
- EI - EMOTIONAL INTELLIGENCE
- S - SMART

"IT'S NOT HOW SMART YOU ARE, IT'S HOW YOU ARE SMART"

IMAGINATION
$I = f(W + S + E + P + R)$

- W - WHAT'S MISSING
- S - SCAMPER
- E - EXTENDED EFFORT PRINCIPLE
- P - PAIN POINTS
- R - READ THE MARKET AND IT'S EDGES

INTEGRATION OF ALL 4

SETTING UP YOUR JOURNAL

My basic Journal setup is purposely quick and simple. After all, I want to be up-and-running with a standard bound blank book as quickly as possible. Nothing stunts the development of a positive habit like unnecessary complexity.

I'm often reminded of a quote from Leonardo Da Vinci:

"Simplicity is the ultimate sophistication."

... which reminds me to keep things simple, so I can enjoy the sophistication later.

You will likely find yourself modifying my suggested template as you spend time journaling, which is great and encouraged!

My specific set-up, particularly the Legend Categories, is created as a jumping-off point. I can assure you it won't be long before you begin to add your own unique reference symbols after noting your own particular needs and habits.

STEP ONE: JOURNAL NUMBER, DATE RANGE, AND OWNERSHIP

When you begin to accumulate multiple journals, including a Number and Date Range on each one of them will become

> "USE YOUR GIFTS FAITHFULLY AND THEY WILL BE ENLARGED; PRACTICE WHAT YOU KNOW, AND YOU SHALL ATTAIN HIGHER KNOWLEDGE."
>
> — MATTHEW ARNOLD

Four Loop Learning: The Art of Journaling and Reflective Leadership

more and more important and extremely handy when referring to previous material. Along with a name and contact information up front, I regularly include the phrase "If found, please return for reward."

STEP TWO:
TAB INVENTORY

On the inside cover of your journal, place tabs of different colors in a neat array. These will be enormously useful for marking pages to which you want instant access to — a great quote, information you want at your fingertips, an idea to which you want to return, etc. You will mark a lot of pages. You might even color-code your tabs if you find that you regularly mark certain sorts of material. I always carry a black Sharpie to write on the tabs for easier search capability.

STEP THREE:
LEGEND CATEGORIES

The Legend Categories are elements you will find yourself personalizing and modifying as you progress in journaling. I've created a "starter set" of categories to get you launched, but it won't be long before you begin seeing recurring themes that demand your own specific references such as training logs,

Setting Up Your Journal

medical visit summaries, collection of leadership best practices, health-related activities, etc.

When referencing something from a past journal, use an arrow-bar symbol like the one on the bottom of the Legend Category page.

The simple formula is *B (Book or Journal number here) : (page number or numbers here)*

> B#: PAGE#

STEP FOUR: PAGE NUMBERING

If your blank Journal does not already have page numbers, be sure to add at least the first 25 to the lower outside corners of each page and add more as you go until you have a fully numbered book.

That's it — you're ready to go!

A custom journal with all the preprinted pages is available to purchase for your convenience on my website at www.FourLoopLearning.com.

IF FOUND, PLEASE RETURN...

About five years ago, after another successful GE Global Customer Summit at the Crotonville campus, I had a car service drop me off at New York's LaGuardia Airport to catch a flight back home to Milwaukee. When I got out of the car, I stepped on something that slightly twisted my ankle — a big fat wallet loaded with lots of credit cards and cash.

I picked up the wallet and took out the driver's license, as the person who lost it was probably having a panic attack wondering where it was and, even worse, how they would get home without money or identification.

With the ID in hand and the lost wallet safely tucked away, I quickly walked around the terminal and soon found an older man sitting on a bench. He had his head in his hands, and tears in his eyes. I walked up to him and asked if he lost something and if he would share his name. I was so happy to be able to say: "Today is your lucky day, because I found your wallet out on the curbside."

The man grabbed his wallet, pulled out all of the bills and handed them to me as a gesture of gratitude, but I asked him gently to keep the money. Being a momentary "hero" was reward enough!

As I reflected on the joy that this man received from a complete stranger, it dawned on me that I would have the same joy if I ever lost one of my valuable journals and it was returned to me. It was on that flight home that evening that the phrase "If Found, Please Return for Reward as This Journal Means an Awful Lot to Me" was formally added to the Journals.

10 CONCLUSION

The goal of journaling is really quite simple. Be just a bit more deliberate in your reflective thinking time so you can put more thoughts and deeper thinking into better and more effective ways of doing things.

I would like to leave you with 5 final thoughts:

FIVE FINAL THOUGHTS

1. START SMALL AND BUILD OVER TIME

Don't worry about being perfect. You will find that after only a few journals, the ability to connect ideas is so much more important than how they look. If you are not sure where to start, try recording your most significant learning every day (or night) for 30 days and then go back and cross reference them to the 3 "H's" of Head, Heart, or Hand. This is a great way to get started and see where and how you are spending your time.

2. ADD INNOVATION TO EVERY NEW JOURNAL

Keep track of your journal improvement ideas as you customize your journal to your life. When you come up with an innovative idea, make sure you date it because as you iterate to make it better you will want to see how your thoughts progressed. This is how I created the Ambition Flowchart, the Health & Happiness

> "YOUR LEVEL OF SUCCESS IS DETERMINED BY YOUR LEVEL OF DISCIPLINE AND PERSEVERANCE."
>
> — ANONYMOUS

> "We first make our habits, and then our habits make us."
> - John Dryden

Check-ups, and the 5-4-3-2-1 networking and conference learning strategy. They all started as little ideas and then dramatically expanded over time, reflection, and usage.

I would be honored if you shared any big journaling ideas you come up with throughout your journaling journey.

3. PRACTICE MAKES PERFECT

Acknowledge that building muscle for intentional journaling can be challenging as most of us default to the old ways of doing things when we are under pressure — and we are *all* under pressure. When journaling is working, persevere and keep it going. When distractions throw you a journaling curveball, try again and pivot back.

Balancing reflection in a world that demands such a strong bias for action will be a constant challenge. Journaling acts as a constant reminder of the value it brings; a personal trove of knowledge to help not only yourself but others enhance leadership skills.

4. ENJOY ACCIDENTAL OR SERENDIPITOUS FINDINGS

Some of my best ideas came from simply connecting the dots between three or four different journals. Sometimes I'll come across a key piece of information from an older journal that has a perfect link to something on working on now—bridging a key learning from yesterday to a better solution today.

Occasionally I will take a journal from a decade ago just to see how much my thinking and perspectives have changed. It makes me realize how much I have learned, yet quickly humbles me when I realize how much *more* there is to learn. This is a constant reminder why leadership development is truly a lifetime journey.

Conclusion

Also, once you get started and learn how to enjoy the benefits of reflective thinking time, it will be hard to stop!

5. FINAL POINT ON NOTE-TAKING AND NOTE-MAKING

The goal of this journal is to share knowledge to help others fulfill their ambitions. The gift of helping others is one of the important reasons I have been journaling for 20 years. It's a great overall feeling of accomplishment and satisfaction when you can help others achieve their potential and goals in life… to me, that's leadership!

> **"I miss the beauty of that blank page, daring you to write on it."**
> **- Bruce Springsteen**

Sharing with others has been a constant theme in the journals and here are a few of my favorite quotes:

"It is in giving that we receive."
St. Francis of Assisi

"Make time for others."
Pope Francis, Journal 34

"The fragrance of the rose is always in the hand that gives it."
Mahatma Gandhi, Journal 37

"Instead, he leaked what he loved…and pretty soon where he stood swallowed us all by the lake it formed."
Bob Dove, Journal 43

"To know even one life has breathed easier because you have lived. This is to have succeeded."
Ralph Waldo Emerson, Journal 64

As you read these quotes I hope that you have a deeper understanding of why I journal and why "teaching a person to fish" can be so meaningful and enjoyable.

Four Loop Learning: The Art of Journaling and Reflective Leadership

The last thing I would like you to remember is this simple formula:

Reflection + Deeper Inspection = Better Direction

Happy Journaling to achieve better directions!

NOTES

Page 34
Locke, John. "An Essay Concerning Human Understanding." Lecture at Columbia University. 1652 Print.

Page 37
Gladwell, Malcolm. *Outliers*. New York, NY: Hachette Book Company, 2008.

Page 37
Newport, John Paul. "The Cost of Being Tiger." Bloomberg Businessweek. May 2018.

Page 41
Allen, David. *Getting Things Done*. London, England: Viking Penguin, 2003

Duhigg, Charles. *The Power of Habit*. New York, NY. Random House. 2014.

Newport, Cal. *Deep Work*. New York, NY. Hachette Book Group. 2016.

Page 42
Bradberry, Travis., and Graves, Jean. *Emotional Intelligence 2.0*. Talentsmart, 2012.

Quinn, Robert E., and V. Anjan. "When Work Has Meaning." Harvard Business Review. July/August 2018.

Left, Joseph., and Ingram, Harrington. Johari Window. 1995

Page 44
Ciampa, Dan. "The More Senior Your Job Title, The More You Need To Keep A Journal." Harvard Business Review. 2017.

Isaksen, Scott G., Dorval, K. Brian, & Treffinger, Donald J. *Creative Approaches To Problem Solving. A Framework For Innovation And Change*. Sage Publications. 2011.

Page 46
Halford, Scott G. *Activate Your Brain*. Austin, TX. Greenleaf Book Group Press. 2015.

Page 46
Mueller, Pam., and Oppenheimer, Daniel. "The Pen Is Mightier Than The Keyboard: Advantages Of Longhand Over Laptop Note Taking." Physiological Science 2014, Vol 25 (6) 1159-1168. Downloaded from pss.sagepub.com at UCLA.

Page 47
Carr, Nicholas. *The Shallows*. New York, NY. Stanford University Press. 2010.

Page 49
Dynarski, Susan. "Laptops are Great. But Not During A Lecture or Meeting." New York Times Article. November 26, 2017.

Page 50
Medina, John J. *Brain Rules*. Seattle, WA. Pear Press. 2008.

Paine, Nigel. *The Learning Challenge: Dealing with Technology, Innovation and Change in Learning and Development*. Philadelphia, PA. Kogan Page Limited. 2014.

Page 85
Porter, Michael E., Noharia, Nitin. "How CEO's Manage Their Time." Harvard Business Review. July/August. 2018.

Page 104
Meister, Jeanne. *Corporate Universities: Lessons in Building a World Class Work Force, Revised Edition*. New York, NY. McGraw-Hill Education. 1998.

Notes

Personalizing 250 journals for a YPO event.